CANDLESTICK CHARTING EXPLAINED

**Timeless Techniques for
Trading Stocks and Futures**

GREGORY L. MORRIS

McGraw-Hill
New York   San Francisco   Washington, D.C.   Auckland   Bogotá
Caracas   Lisbon   London   Madrid   Mexico City   Milan
Montreal   New Delhi   San Juan   Singapore
Sydney   Tokyo   Toronto

W9-AYW-733

McGraw-Hill

A Division of The McGraw-Hill Companies

© 1992, 1995 Gregory L. Morris

Originally published as CandlePower

All rights reserved. No part of this publication may be reproduced, stored in a retrieval system, or transmitted, in any form or by any means, electronic, mechanical, photocopying, recording, or otherwise, without the prior written permission of the publisher.

ISBN 1–55738–891–1

Printed in the United States of America
14 13   04 03 02

Dedicated to
Candis, Dusti, and Grant;
three of my brightest candles.

Table of Contents

Table of Contents

Foreword

I am a collector of first editions of books. My specialties include astronomy texts written before 1900, such as Percival Lowell's classic *Mars*, the first published speculations about the possibility of life on the red planet (which inspired Jules Verne to write *The War of the Worlds*), and a strange little tome from 1852 that claims astronomer William Hershel spotted sheep on the Moon with his telescope.

My collection also includes about 200 business books written by authors I have interviewed through the years. My inscribed copy of Ivan Boesky's *Merger Mania*, for example, was appraised a few years ago at $200.

But my sentimental favorite is a beat-up old chart book of the Dow Jones Industrials and Transportations Averages going back to December 18, 1896, the day the modern Dow Jones averages were born. (Trivia question: Where did the Dow Industrials close after its very first day of trading? Answer: 38.59.) Back then, the Industrials only had 12 components, and the Transports, with 20 issues, were known as the Rails.

A 90-year-old FNN viewer from Virginia offered it to me in the fall of 1985.

"I have been interested in, but not too active in, the market since the early '20's," he wrote, "and lived through the '29 'break' and the great depression which was a 'tempering' influence against excessive enthusiasm.

"At age 90 my activities are confined to 'growth' stocks and safe investments. I am no longer interested in 'speculation.'" So he wondered if I would be interested in his chart book.

Indeed, I was. I gladly accepted in exchange for a signed copy of one of Joe Granville's books.

The book was published in 1931 by Robert Rhea, the famed disciple of Charles Dow and of the oldest form of technical analysis, the Dow Theory. It covers the years 1896–1948, with each page devoted to one year's trading of both averages.

It is one big faded green rectangle, measuring 11 inches high and 18 inches across. Its heavy cardboard covers are held together by a couple of rusty screws.

I browse through it once in awhile, marveling at its simplicity. Each day's closing value is designated by a single horizontal hash mark meticulously notched on the graph paper. Nothing fancy. No intra-day highs and lows, no trendlines, no points or figures; just a simple daily record of the debits and credits of civilization.

There is the market panic in December of 1899, when the Industrials plunged from 76 to 58 in just 13 trading days.

There is the period from July to December of 1914, when, incredibly, the market was closed on account of World War I. Eerily, half the page devoted to that year is blank.

And, of course, there is 1929, when the Industrials peaked on September 3 at 381.17 and hit bottom, three pages later, in July of 1932 at 41.22.

The book means a lot to me. Between its covers there is a bit of history, some mathematics, a dose of economics, and a dash of psychology. It has taught me much about a discipline that I once considered voodoo.

Good journalists are supposed to maintain an open mind about the stories they cover. Political reporters, for example, should be neither Republican nor Democrat. And successful financial reporters should avoid being either bullish or bearish. And they should also be familiar with both fundamental and technical analysis.

I remember the first time I interviewed a technical market analyst in the fall of 1981, when I was still cutting my teeth on business news. This analyst spoke of 34-day and 54-week market cycles and head-and-shoulder bottoms and wedge formations. I thought it was so much mumbo-jumbo until the summer of '82 when the bull market was launched, and the fundamental analysts were still bemoaning the depths of the recession that gripped the economy at the time. That was when I realized the technicians may have something there.

He doesn't know it, but Greg Morris taught me a lot about technical analysis. Or, more accurately, his N-Squared software did. For a couple years during the mid-80's, I hand-entered the daily NYSE advance/decline readings and the closing figures of a few market indices into my computer. I used N-Squared to build charts and draw trendlines. (I hadn't yet learned about modems and down-loading from databanks.)

The slow, painstaking process gave me a hands on, almost organic, feel for the markets. And watching various repetitive chart patterns unfold on the computer screen was a great lesson about supply and demand and about market psychology.

I think I understand how technical analysis works. It's the *why* that still puzzles me. I understand the supply and demand implications of support and resistance levels, for example, and I appreciate the theories behind pennant formations and rising bottoms.

But I still marvel at what ultimately makes technical analysis work: that intangible *something* that causes technicians to anthropomorphize the markets without even realizing it. The market is tired, they say. Or the market is trying to tell us this or that. Or the market always knows the news before the newspapers do.

That *something*, in my mind, is simply the human side of the market, which I suggest American technicians tend to ignore. Technical analysis is, after all, as much art as it is science. But too many analysts have a mathematical blind spot, and I blame that on computers. Yes, charts represent numerical relationships. But they also depict human perceptions and behavior.

Enter Sakata's Candlesticks, which combine the highly quantitative ratiocination of American technical analysis with the intuitive elegance of

Foreword

Japanese philosophy. Greg Morris has more than ably turned his attention to this fascinating charting style with this book.

It occurs to me that Japanese Candlesticks are the perfect form of technical analysis for the '90's. I happen to agree with authors John Naisbett and Patricia Aburdene. In their bestseller *Megatrends 2000*, they write that we're headed for the age of spirituality. It won't necessarily be an overtly religious period, mind you, but rather one subtle, intuitive power we may all develop that allows us to sense things before they actually happen. It will be a period that embraces a kind of hybrid Eastern philosophy and Western practicality without all the New Age hocus-pocus.

Just right for Candlestick analysis. The system is precise and exacting, but it charms with its haiku-like names for chart patterns: "paper umbrella," or "spinning tops," for example.

But I'll let Greg Morris tell the story from here. I just hope my 90-year old friend is still around to read it. I think he would like it.

Bill Griffeth, Anchor
"Strictly Business," CNBC
Park Ridge, NJ

Preface

Japanese candlestick charting and analysis is definitely a viable and effective tool for stock and commodity market timing and analysis. That is a bold statement, especially when you consider the universe of analysis techniques that are being promoted, offered, sold, used, abused, and touted. Other than Nison's work, the only problem has been the lack of detailed information on how to use and identify them. Not only will this book solve this problem, but it will also provoke an intellectual curiosity in candlesticks that will not easily disappear.

Japanese candlesticks provide visual insight into current market psychology. There is no ancient mystery behind Japanese candlesticks, as some promoters would have you believe. They are, however, a powerful method for analyzing and timing the stock and futures markets. That they have been used for hundreds of years only supports that fact. When candlesticks are combined with other technical indicators, market timing and trading results can be enhanced considerably.

It is almost regretful that this sound analysis technique was introduced to the West using the word "candlesticks" instead of some more appealing or appropriate terminology, such as Sakata's Methods or Sakata's Five Methods. If candlesticks' Western debut had focused on the uncovering of an ancient Japanese analysis technique called Sakata's Methods, I believe their acceptance would have been quicker and more widespread. None of this, however, changes the contribution that candlesticks make to technical analysis, only fewer misleading claims would have been made.

In January 1992, I completed a week of study in Japan with Mr. Takehiro Hikita, an independent and active futures trader. While staying in his home, we thoroughly discussed the entire realm of Japanese culture related to candlestick analysis. His extensive knowledge and dedication to the subject made my learning experience not only enjoyable, but quite thorough. His insistence that I try to understand the psychology at the same time was instrumental in learning many of the pattern concepts. I hope that I have transposed that priceless information into this book.

This is a book that not only covers the basics, but offers more detail into exactly how to identify and use the patterns. A comprehensive analysis and recognition methodology will be presented so that you will have no doubt in your mind when you see a candlestick pattern. In addition to a thorough coverage of the candlestick patterns, the philosophy of their use will be discussed so that you will have a complete understanding of Japanese candle pattern analysis and its usefulness to market timing and strategies. Candle patterns need to be defined within parameters that people can understand and use in their everyday analysis. This can still involve flexibility as long as the limits of that flexibility are defined, or at least explained.

An attempt to take the subjectivity out of Japanese candlesticks analysis will be a primary thrust of this book. Most sources that deal with candlesticks admit that patterns should be taken into the context of the market. This is true, but is often an excuse to avoid the complicated methodology of pattern recognition.

Chapters on statistical testing and evaluation will reveal, totally, all assumptions used and all details of the testing results. Rigorous testing has been done on stocks, futures, and indices. Some of the results were surprising and some were predictable. All results are shown for your use and perusal.

There is nothing more tiring, useless, and inefficient than reading page after page of detailed analysis on chart patterns about how the market was or what you should have done. The seemingly endless verbiage about how you would have done if you had only recognized this or that when this or that occurred is totally worthless. Charting examples will be shown in this book only as learning examples of the candle patterns being discussed. It definitely helps to see the actual candle patterns using real data.

I could not have allowed myself even to start a project as involved as this if I had even the slightest doubt as to the viability and credibility of using Japanese candlesticks as an additional tool for market analysis and timing. Over the last fifteen years, I have read almost every book on technical analysis, used every type of indicator, followed numerous analysts, and developed technical and economic analysis software in association with N-Squared Computing. Believe me, if candlesticks were just a passing fancy, this book would not have been considered — certainly not by me.

I felt that a straightforward approach in writing the book would be the most accepted, and certainly the most believable. When I buy a book to learn about a new technique, a textbook-like approach is appreciated. Hence, this style has played a vital part in the structure and organization of this book.

This book will not only introduce and explain all of the inner workings of Japanese candlesticks, but will also serve as a reference manual for later use. Each candle pattern has been defined and explained in a standard format so that quick and easy referral is possible. I will introduce a new method of analysis called "candlestick filtering," which, based upon my research, is essential for better recognition. You will see it gain in popularity because it can provide such a sound basis for future analysis and research.

Japanese candlestick analysis used with other technical/market indicators will improve your performance and understanding of the markets. Even if you use candlesticks solely as a method of displaying data, you will find them indispensable. Candlestick charting, candle pattern analysis, and candlestick filtering will give you an edge, a tool if you will, that will enhance your understanding of the markets and trading performance. Learn CandlePower, use it, enjoy its rewards.

Greg Morris
Dallas, Texas

Acknowledgments

There are people without whom this book could not have been possible. Where do I start? Who do I mention first? This, quite possibly, is more difficult than the book itself.

One must never forget one's roots. There is no doubt in my mind that my parents, Dwight and Mary Morris, are mostly responsible for all the good that I have ever accomplished. Any of the bad surely had to come from being a jet fighter pilot in the U.S. Navy for six years.

I am blessed with a wonderful wife and children. Their support during this effort was unwavering and fully appreciated.

Norman North (Mr. N-Squared Computing) has gone from a business associate to a valued friend. His insight and opinions are always sought and usually relied upon. The bottom line is this: without Norm, this book would not have been written.

I am forever grateful to Takehiro Hikita for his gracious offer to visit Japan, stay in his home, and help with the many Japanese interpretations. My trip to Japan in January 1992 to study Japanese candlestick analysis was invaluable. His knowledge of candle pattern analysis is filtered throughout this book.

I cannot forget the fact that John Bollinger, while at a Market Technicians Association meeting in Phoenix in 1988, said that I should look into candlesticks. I have; thanks, John.

Acknowledgments

Ron Salter, of Salter Asset Management, has always offered an unusual but insightful opinion on the economy and the markets; one that usually seems to be more right than wrong. I am grateful for his permission to quote some of his comments from his client letter.

Steve Nison must be given full credit and acknowledgment for pioneering "candlesticks" into Western analysis. His book *Japanese Candlestick Charting Techniques,* published by New York Institute of Finance / Simon & Schuster is a classic and provides the reader with a rich history of candlesticks and candlestick analysis. Nison coined many of the English names for the various patterns used in the West today.

Many of the concepts used in the West today originated from Nison's work and have been widely accepted as commonplace among candlestick enthusiasts. This book does not try to change that.

The first book translated into English about Japanese candlesticks was *The Japanese Chart of Charts,* by Seiki Shimizu. This book provided an immense wealth of information about all of the popular candle patterns along with their many interpretations. It was translated by Greg Nicholson.

Another valuable source of information on candlesticks was published by Nippon Technical Analysts Association, called *Analysis of Stock Prices in Japan,* 1988.

My thanks also go to Commodity Systems, Inc. and Track Data Corp. for the use of their stock and commodity databases.

As is the accepted standard, and certainly in this case the fact, whatever factual errors and omissions are sadly, but most certainly, my own.

1 | Introduction

Japanese candlestick analysis is a valid form of technical analysis and should be treated as such. Promoters of instant wealth will always misdirect and abuse their rights, but in the end, they are not around long enough to cause any substantial damage. One should always look into any new technique with a healthy amount of skepticism. Hopefully, this book will keep that skepticism under control and unnecessary.

Technical Analysis

When considering technical analysis, one should remember that things are quite often not always what they seem. Many facts that we learned are not actually true; and what seems to be the obvious, sometimes is not. Many people believe water runs out of a bathtub faster as it gets to the end. Some people may drink like a fish, but fish don't drink. George Washington neither cut down a cherry tree, nor threw a dollar across the Potomac. Dogs don't sweat through their tongues, Audi automobiles never mysteriously accelerated, and the Battle of Bunker Hill was not fought at Bunker Hill.

A good detective will tell you that some of the least reliable information comes from eye witnesses. When people observe an event, it seems their background, education, and other influences, color their perception of what occurred. A most important thing that detectives try to do at a crime scene, is to prevent the observers from talking to each other, because most will be influenced by what others say they saw.

Another curious human failing becomes a factor when we observe facts. The human mind does not handle large numbers or macro ideas well. That thousands of people die each year from automobile accidents raises scarcely an eyebrow, but one airplane crash killing only a few people, grabs the nation. We are only modestly concerned that tens of thousands of people are infected with AIDS, but we are touched deeply when presented with an innocent child that has been indirectly infected. If a situation is personalized, we can focus on it. We can become deluded by our emotions, and these emotions can effect our perceptions. When our portfolios are plunging, all of the fears that we can imagine are dragged out: recession, debt, war, budget, bank failures, etc. Something is needed to keep us from falling victim to everyday emotion and delusion; that something is technical analysis.

Almost all methods of technical analysis generate useful information, which if used for nothing more than uncovering and organizing facts about market behavior, will increase the investor's understanding of the markets. The investor is made painfully aware that technical competence does not ensure competent trading. Speculators who lose money do so not only because of bad analysis, but because of their inability to transform their analysis into sound practice. Bridging the vital gap between analysis and action requires overcoming the threats of fear, greed and hope. It means controlling impatience and the desire to stray away from a sound method to something new during times of temporary adversity. It means having the discipline to believe what you see and to follow the indications from sound methods, even though they contradict what everyone else is saying or what seems to be the correct course of action.

Japanese Candlestick Analysis

As a new and exciting dimension of technical analysis, Japanese candlestick charting and candle pattern analysis will help anyone who wishes to have another tool at their disposal; a tool that will help sort and control the constant disruptions and continued outside influences to sound stock and futures market analysis.

What does candlestick charting offer that typical Western high-low bar charts do not? As far as actual data displayed—nothing. However, when it comes to visual appeal and the ability to see data relationships easier, candlesticks are exceptional. A quick insight to the recent trading psychology is there before you. After a minimal amount of practice and familiarization, candlesticks will become part of your analysis arsenal. You may never return to standard bar charts.

Japanese candlesticks offer a quick picture into the psychology of short-term trading, studying the effect, not the cause. This places candlesticks squarely into the category of technical analysis. One cannot ignore the fact that prices are influenced by investor's psychologically driven emotions of fear, greed, and hope. The overall psychology of the marketplace cannot be measured by statistics; some form of technical analysis must be used to analyze the changes in these psychological factors. Japanese candlesticks read the changes in the makeup of investor's interpretations of value. This is then reflected in price movement. More than just a method of pattern recognition, candlesticks show the interaction between buyers and sellers. Japanese candlestick charting provides insight into the financial markets that is not readily available with other charting methods. It works well with either stocks or commodities. Related analysis techniques, such as candlestick filtering and CandlePower charting, will add to your analysis and timing capabilities.

This book not only will serve as an introduction to Japanese candlestick charting and analysis, but will also provide conclusive evidence of the usefulness of candlestick patterns as an analysis tool. All methods of analysis and all assumptions will be open and unobstructed. You will, after reading this book, either begin to use candlesticks to assist in your market analysis and timing or be confident enough in them to further your own research into candlestick analysis.

Japanese Candlesticks and You

Once you become accustomed to using candlestick charts, you will find it disconcerting to be limited to a standard bar chart. Without candlesticks, you will feel that you are not seeing the complete picture — that something is missing. Besides providing the quick and easy pattern recognition, candlesticks have great visual appeal. The data relationships almost jump off the page (or computer screen), hardly the case with bar charts.

Candlestick Charts versus Bar Charts

Throughout this book, the assumed time period, will be a single day of trading. It should be understood that a bar or candle line can represent any trading period, not always just a day. However, daily analysis is probably the most common and will thus represent the period of trading for this book. Additionally, the mention of investors, speculators, and traders will be used throughout with no attempt to classify or define them.

Standard Bar Charts

The data required to produce a standard bar chart consists of the open, high, low, and close prices for the time period under study. A bar chart consists of vertical lines representing the high to low range in prices for that day. The high price refers to the highest price that the issue traded during that day. Likewise, the low price refers to the lowest price traded that day.

Figure 1-1

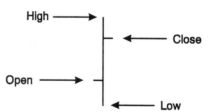

4

For years, the only other price element used in bar charting was the close price. The close was represented on the high-low bar as a small tick mark extending from the bar out to the right. Recently, bar charting has incorporated the open price by another small tick on the left side of the high-low bar. This stands true for almost all stock charts and stock data vendors. Most futures and commodity charts have always used the open price because it was more readily available.

Figure 1-2

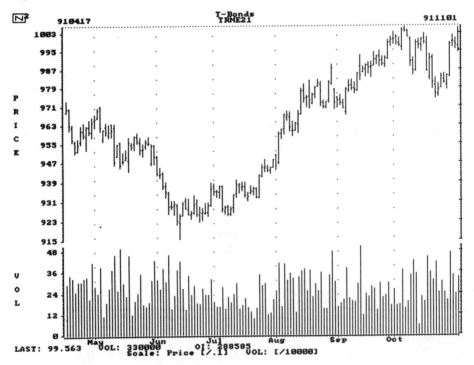

Most bar charts are displayed with a volume histogram at the bottom. Charting services also offer a number of popular indicators along with the bar chart. Technical analysis software vendors gave the user a great deal of flexibility in displaying the bar charts. The standard bar chart could be displayed with indicators, volume, open interest, and a large assortment of other technical tools appropriate for that software.

Candlestick Charts

Japanese candlestick charts do not require anything new or different as far as data are concerned. Open, high, low, and close are all that is needed to do candlestick charting. Many data vendors do not have open prices on stocks. This problem can be addressed by using the previous day's close for today's open price. This, however, presents a somewhat controversial situation and is thoroughly discussed in Chapter 6.

The Body (*jittai*)

The box that makes up the difference between the open and close is called the real body of the candlestick. The height of the body is the range between the day's open price and the day's close price. When this body is black, it means that the closing price was lower than the opening price. When the closing price is higher than the opening, the body is white.

Figure 1-3

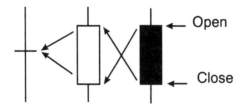

The Shadows (*kage*)

The candlestick line may have small thin lines above and/or below the body. These lines are called shadows and represent the high and low prices reached during the trading day. The upper shadow (*uwakage*) represents the high price and the lower shadow (*shitakage*) represents the low price. Some Japanese traders refer to the upper shadow as the hair and the lower shadow as the tail. It is these shadows that give the appearance of a candle and its wick(s).

When drawing candlestick charts by hand, the Japanese use red instead of white to represent the up days (close higher than open). With the use of computers, this is not feasible because red would be printed as black on most printers and you could not tell the up days from the down days. This also applies to photocopying.

Figure 1-4

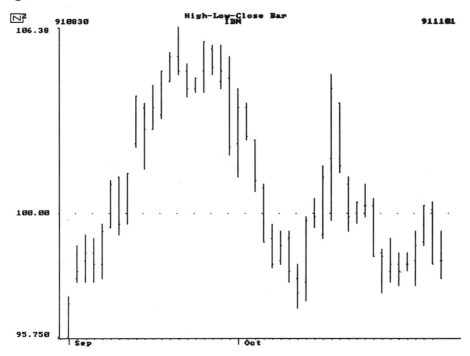

High-Low-Close Bar
IBM

If you compare Figures 1-4 and 1-5, you can see that the Japanese candlestick chart really does not display anything different from the standard bar chart. However, once you become accustomed to seeing Japanese candlestick charts, you will prefer them because their clarity is superior and allows a quick and accurate interpretation of the data. This matter of interpretation is also what this book is about. Japanese candlestick charting and analysis will continue to grow and gain in popularity. For as long as it is used as intended, only a profit of doom would suggest its demise.

Chapter 1

Figure 1-5

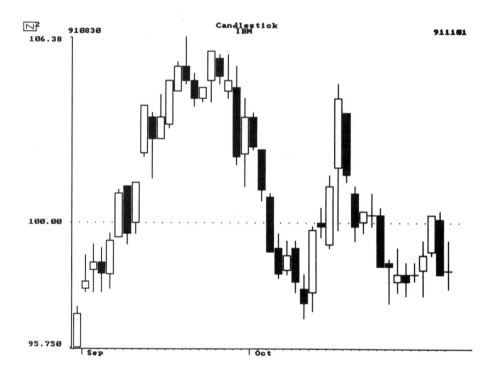

2 | Candlestick Lines

A day of trading in any stock or futures market is represented in traditional charts by a single line or price bar; Japanese candlestick charting is no different, except that the information is so much more easily interpreted.

There is much information provided in a single candle line. This will help in understanding the psychology behind the many candle patterns described in later chapters. There are a few candle patterns that consist of only a single candlestick and also qualify as reversal patterns. They will be covered thoroughly in the chapter on reversal patterns.

Each type of candle line has a unique name and represents a possible trading scenario for that day. Some candle lines have Japanese names and some have English names. Whenever possible, if the name is in English, the Japanese name will also be given. The Japanese name will be written in a form called Romanji. This is a method of writing Japanese so that it can be pronounced properly by non-Japanese-speaking people. Single candle lines are often referred to as yin and yang lines. The terms yin and yang are Chinese, but have been used by Western analysts to account for polar terms, such as in/out, on/off, up/down, and over/under. (The Japanese equivalents are *inn* and *yoh*.) Yin relates to bearish and yang relates to bullish. There are nine basic yin and yang lines in candlestick analysis. These can be expanded to fifteen different candle lines for a clearer explanation of the various possibilities. It will be shown in later chapters how most candle patterns can be reduced to single candle lines and maintain the same bullish or bearish connotations.

Reading the single daily lines is the beginning of Japanese candlestick analysis. A few definitions should be given first. Remember, these terms and descriptions all refer to only a single day of trading. Depictions of candle lines and candle patterns will use a shaded day to show when body color, black or white, is not important.

Long Days

Figure 2-1

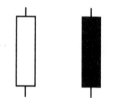

Reference to long days is prevalent in most literature dealing with Japanese candlesticks. Long describes the length of the candlestick body, the difference between the open price and the close price, as shown in Figure 2-1. A long day represents a large price movement for the day. In other words, the open price and close price were considerably different.

How much must the open and close prices differ to qualify as a long day? Like most forms of analysis, context must be considered. Long compared to what? It is best to consider only the most recent price action to determine what is long and what is not. Japanese candlestick analysis is based solely upon the short term price movement so the determination of long days should be also. Anywhere from the previous five to ten days should be more than adequate to produce the proper results. Other acceptable methods of determining long days may also be used. These will be thoroughly discussed in the chapter on pattern identification and recognition.

Short Days

Figure 2-2

Short days, shown in Figure 2-2, may also be based on the same methodology as long days, with comparable results. There are also numerous days that do not fall into any of these two categories.

Marubozu

Marubozu means close-cropped or close-cut in Japanese. Other interpretations refer to it as Bald or Shaven Head. In either case, the meaning reflects the fact that there is no shadow extending from the body at either the open or the close, or at both.

Black Marubozu

Figure 2-3

A Black Marubozu is a long black body with no shadows on either end (Figure 2-3). This is considered an extremely weak line. It often becomes part of a bearish continuation or bullish reversal candle pattern, especially if it occurs during a downtrend. This line, being black, shows the weakness of the continuing downtrend. A long black line could be a final sell off; this is why it is often the first day of many bullish reversal patterns. It is also called a Major Yin or Marubozu of Yin.

White Marubozu

Figure 2-4

A White Marubozu is a long white body with no shadows on either end. This is an extremely strong line when considered on its own merits. Opposite of the Black Marubozu, it often is the first part of a bullish continuation or bearish reversal candle pattern. It is sometimes called a Major Yang or Marubozu of Yang.

Closing Marubozu

Figure 2-5

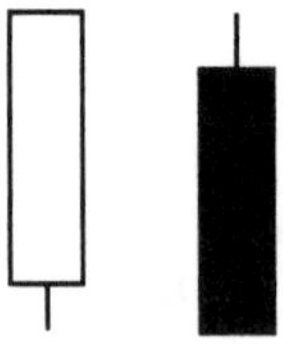

A Closing Marubozu has no shadow extending from the close end of the body, whether the body is white or black (Figure 2-5). If the body is white, there is no upper shadow because the close is at the top of the body. Likewise, if the body is black, there is no lower shadow because the close is at the bottom of the body. The Black Closing Marubozu (*yasunebike*) is considered a weak line and the White Closing Marubozu is a strong line.

Opening Marubozu

The Opening Marubozu has no shadow extending from the open price end of the body (Figure 2-6). If the body is white, there would be no lower shadow, making it a strong bullish line. The Black Opening Marubozu (*yoritsuki takane*), with no upper shadow, is a weak and therefore bearish line. The Opening Marubozu is not as strong as the Closing Marubozu.

Figure 2-6

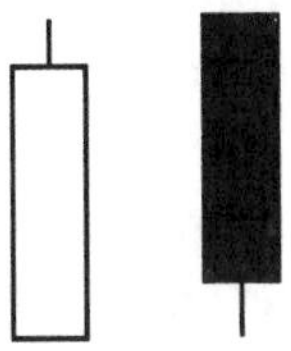

Spinning Tops (*koma*)

Figure 2-7

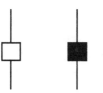

Spinning Tops are candlestick lines that have small real bodies with upper and lower shadows that are of greater length than the body's length. This represents indecision between the bulls and the bears. The color of the body of a spinning top, along with the actual size of the shadows is not important. The small body relative to the shadows is what makes the spinning top.

Doji

When the body of a candle line is so small that the open and closing prices are equal, they are called Doji (simultaneous or concurrent) lines. A Doji occurs when the open and close for that day are the same, or certainly very close to being the same. The lengths of the shadows can vary. The perfect Doji day has the same opening and closing price, however, there is some interpretation that must be considered. Requiring that the open and close be exactly equal would put too much of a constraint on the data and there would not be many Doji. If the difference between the open and close prices is within a few ticks (minimum trading increments), it is more than satisfactory.

Determining a Doji day is similar to the method used for identification of a long day; there are no rigid rules, only guidelines. Just like the long day, it depends upon previous prices. If the previous days were mostly Doji, then the Doji day is not important. If the Doji occurs alone, it's a signal that there is indecision and must not be ignored. In almost all cases, a Doji by itself would not be significant enough to forecast a change in the trend of prices, only a warning of impending trend change. A Doji preceeded by a long white day in an uptrend would be meaningful. This particular combination of days is referred to as a bearish Doji Star (Chapter 3). An uptrend that, all of a sudden, ceases to continue, would be cause for concern. A Doji means that there is uncertainty and indecision.

According to Nison, Doji tend to be better at indicating a change of trend when they occur at tops instead of at bottoms. This is related to the fact that for an uptrend to continue, new buying must be present. A downtrend can continue unabated. It is interesting to note that Doji also means "goof" or "bungle."

Long-Legged Doji (juji)

Figure 2-8

The Long-Legged Doji has long upper and lower shadows in the middle of the day's trading range, clearly reflecting the indecision of buyers and sellers (Figure 2-8). Throughout the day, the market moved higher and then sharply lower, or vice versa. It then closed at or very near the opening price. If the opening and closing are in the center of the day's range, the line is referred to as a Long-Legged Doji. *Juji* means "cross."

Gravestone Doji (*tohba*)

The Gravestone Doji (*hakaishi*), shown in figure 2-9, is another form of a Doji day. It develops when the Doji is at, or very near, the low of the day.

Figure 2-9

The Gravestone Doji, like many of the Japanese terms, is based on various analogies. In this case, the Gravestone Doji represents the graves of those who have died in battle.

If the upper shadow is quite long, it means that the Gravestone Doji is much more bearish. Prices open and trade higher all day only to close where they opened, which is also the low price for the day. This cannot possibly be interpreted as anything but a failure to rally. The Gravestone Doji at a market top is a specific version of a Shooting Star (Chapter 3). The only difference is that the Shooting Star has a small body and the Gravestone Doji, being a Doji, has no body. Some Japanese sources claim that the Gravestone Doji can occur only on the ground, not in the air. This means it can be a bullish indication on the ground or at a market low, not as good as a bearish one. It certainly portrays a sense of indecision and a possible change in trend.

Dragonfly Doji (*tonbo*)

Figure 2-10

The Dragonfly Doji, or Tonbo (pronounced *tombo*), occurs when the open and close are at the high of the day (Figure 2-10). Like other Doji days, this one normally appears at market turning points. You will see in later chapters that this Doji is a special case of the Hanging Man and Hammer lines. A tonbo line with a very long lower shadow (tail) (*shitahige*) is also called a Takuri line. A Takuri line at the end of a downtrend is extremely bullish.

Four Price Doji

Figure 2-11

—

This rare Doji line occurs when all four price components are equal. That is, the open, high, low, and close are the same (Figure 2-11). This line could occur when a stock is very illiquid or the data source did not have any prices other than the close. Futures traders should not confuse this with a limit move. It is so rare that one should suspect data errors. However, it does represent complete and total uncertainty by traders in market direction.

Stars (*hoshi*)

Figure 2-12

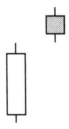

A Star appears whenever a small body gaps above or below the previous day's long body (Figure 2-12). Ideally, the gap should encompass the shadows, but this is not always necessary. A Star indicates some uncertainty in the marketplace. Stars are part of many candle patterns, primarily reversal patterns.

Paper Umbrella (*karakasa*)

Figure 2-13

Many of these lines are also included in the next chapter on candle patterns. Like the previously mentioned candle lines, the Umbrella lines have strong reversal implications. There is strong similarity between the Dragonfly Doji and this candle line. Two of the Umbrella lines are called Hammer and Hanging Man, depending upon their location in the trend of the market.

Conclusion

The single candle lines are essential to Japanese candlestick analysis. When they are used by themselves, and then in combinations with other candle lines, a complete psyche of the market unfolds. Much of the analysis of these lines and patterns is part of Sakata's Method (Chapter 5). However, this book will go beyond the Sakata Method with additional patterns and methods. Some of these patterns are new; some are variations of the originals.

3 | Reversal Candle Patterns

A candle pattern can be a single candlestick line or multiple candlestick lines, seldom more than five or six. In Japanese literature, there is occasional reference to patterns that use even more candlesticks, but they will be included in the chapter on candle formations. The order in which the candle patterns are discussed does not reflect their importance or predictive ability. They are listed in order of their frequency of occurrence, with related patterns following.

Most of the candle patterns are inversely related. That is, for each bullish pattern, there is a similar bearish pattern. The primary difference is their position relative to the short-term trend of the market. The names of the bullish and bearish patterns may or may not be different. So that this chapter can serve as a reference, each pattern set will be covered using the same basic format. Some patterns retain their Japanese names while others have been given English interpretations. A few are identical in construction, but have different names. Any differences will be dealt with in the discussion.

Three small vertical lines will precede the pattern drawing. These lines only show the previous trend of the market and should not be used as immediate reference to pattern relationships.

Reversal versus Continuation Patterns

Reversal and continuation patterns have been separated into different chapters. This chapter covers the reversal patterns and Chapter 4 covers the continuation patterns. This separation was done to add convenience and simplify future reference. This is mentioned here because the determination of bullish or bearish implications has to do only with continued price action and not with previous action. Previous price movement helps to determine only the pattern, not its ability to foresee or anticipate future price movement. Whether a reversal pattern or a continuation pattern, investment and trading decisions still need to be made, even if it is the fact that you decide to do nothing. Chapter 6 deals with this concept at length.

There is a normal expectancy to have a bullish pattern or situation prior to a bearish counterpart. That tendency will continue here, except when one counterpart tends to exhibit greater prevalence; then it will be covered first.

Chapter Format

Most of the candle patterns will be explained using a standard format that should ensure easy reference at a later date. Some candle patterns will not be covered as thoroughly as others because of their simplicity or similarity to other patterns. Some patterns are only modified versions of another pattern, and will be noted as such. Since many patterns have a counterpart reflecting the other side of the market, some of the scenarios will contain only one example. Additionally, some repetition may seem to occur. This too is done so that later reference will be both easy and thorough. The usual format will be:

- **Pattern name**

- **Japanese name and interpretation**
  The romanized Japanese name and meaning, if known
  Comment on whether confirmation is required or suggested

- **Commentary**
  Description of pattern(s)
  Western (traditional) counterpart(s)

- **Graphic of classic pattern(s)**
  Detailed drawing of the classic pattern (days that can be either black or white are shown with shading)

- **Rules of recognition**
  Simplistic rules for quick identification
  Criteria for pattern recognition

- **Scenarios / psychology behind the pattern**
  Possible trading scenarios that could have developed
  General discussion of the psychology of each day

- **Pattern flexibility**
  Situations that change the pattern's effectiveness
  Allowable deviations from the classic pattern
  Information for the numerically oriented and computer programmer

- **Pattern breakdown**
  Reducing the pattern to a single candle line

- **Related Patterns**
  Patterns that have similar formations
  Patterns that are a part of this pattern

- **Examples**

Chapter 3

Index of Reversal Patterns

Hammer and Hanging Man

(*kanazuchi/tonkachi and kubitsuri*)
Confirmation is definitely required.

Figure 3-1   **Figure 3-2**

Commentary

The Hammer and Hanging Man are each made of single candlestick lines (Figures 3-1 and 3-2). They have long lower shadows and small real bodies that are at or very near the top of their daily trading range. These were first introduced as paper umbrellas in Chapter 2. They are also special versions of the Tonbo/Takuri lines.

The Hammer occurs in a downtrend and is so named because it is hammering out a bottom. The Japanese word for Hammer (*tonkachi*) also means the ground or the soil.

A Hanging Man occurs at the top of a trend or during an uptrend. The name Hanging Man (*kubitsuri*) comes from the fact that this candle line looks somewhat like a man hanging.

Another candle line similar to the Hammer is the Takuri (pronounced taguri) line. This Japanese word equates with climbing a rope or hauling up. The motion is not smooth and could be related to pulling up an anchor with your hands: as you change hands, the upward movement is interrupted momentarily. A Takuri line has a lower shadow at least three times the length of the body, whereas the lower shadow of a Hammer is a minimum of only twice the length of the body.

Rules of Recognition

1. The small real body is at the upper end of the trading range.

2. The color of the body is not important.

3. The long lower shadow should be much longer than the length of the real body, usually two to three times.

4. There should be no upper shadow, or if there is, it should be very small.

Scenarios and Psychology Behind the Pattern

Hammer

The market has been in a downtrend, so there is an air of bearishness. The market opens and then sells off sharply. However, the sell-off is abated and the market returns to, or near, its high for the day. The failure of the market to continue the selling reduces the bearish sentiment, and most traders will be uneasy with any bearish positions they might have. If the close is above the open, causing a white body, the situation is even better for the bulls. Confirmation would be a higher open with yet a still higher close on the next trading day.

Hanging Man

For the Hanging Man, the market is considered bullish because of the uptrend. In order for the Hanging Man to appear, the price action for the day must trade much lower than where it opened, then rally to close near the high. This is what causes the long lower shadow which shows how the market just might begin a sell-off. If the market opens lower the next day, there would be many participants with long positions that would want to look for an opportunity to sell. Steve Nison claims that a confirmation that the Hanging Man is bearish might be that the body is black and the next day opens lower.

Pattern Flexibility

Features that will enhance the signal of a Hammer or Hanging Man pattern are an extra long lower shadow, no upper shadow, very small real body (almost Doji), the preceding sharp trend and a body color that reflects the opposite sentiment (previous trend). This trait, when used on the Hammer, will change its name to a Takuri line. Takuri lines are, generally, more bullish than Hammers.

The body color of the Hanging Man and the Hammer can add to the significance of the pattern's predictive ability. A Hanging Man with a black body is more bearish than one with a white body. Likewise, a Hammer with a white body would be more bullish than one with a black body.

As with most single candlestick patterns like the Hammer and the Hanging Man, it is important to wait for confirmation. This confirmation may merely be the action on the open of the next day. Many times, though, it is best to wait for a confirming close on the following day. That is, if a Hammer is shown, the following day should close even higher before bullish positions are taken.

The lower shadow should be, at a minimum, twice as long as the body, but not more than three times. The upper shadow should be no more than 5 to 10 percent of the high-low range. The low of the body should be below the trend for a Hammer and above the trend for a Hanging Man.

Pattern Breakdown

The Hammer and Hanging Man patterns, being single candle lines, cannot be reduced further. See Paper Umbrella in Chapter 2.

Related Patterns

The Hammer and Hanging Man are special cases of the Dragonfly Doji discussed in the previous chapter. In most instances, the Dragonfly Doji would be more bearish than the Hanging Man.

Examples

Figure 3-3A

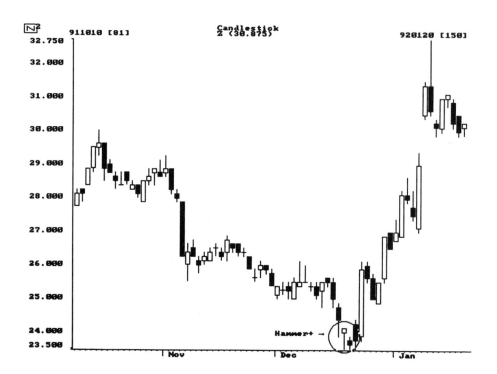

Figure 3-3B

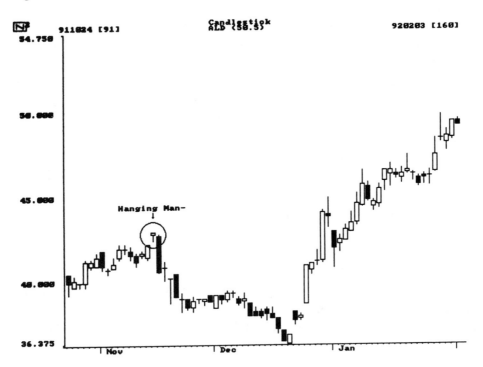

Engulfing

(*tsutsumi*)
Confirmation is suggested.

Figure 3-4

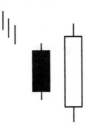

Figure 3-5

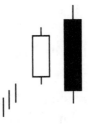

27

Commentary

The Engulfing pattern consists of two real bodies of opposite color (Figures 3-4 and 3-5). The second day's body completely engulfs the prior day's body. The shadows are not considered in this pattern. It is also called the Embracing (*daki*) line because it embraces the previous day's line. When this occurs near a market top, or in an uptrend, it indicates a shifting of the sentiment to selling. A Yin Tsutsumi after an uptrend is called the Final Daki line and is one of the Sakata techniques discussed in a later chapter.

The first day of the Engulfing pattern has a small body and the second day has a long real body. Because the second day's move is so much more dramatic, it reflects a possible end to the previous trend. If the bearish Engulfing pattern appears after a sustained move, it increases the chance that most bulls are already long. In this case, there may not be enough new money (bulls) to keep the market uptrend intact.

An Engulfing pattern is similar to the traditional outside day. Just like the Engulfing pattern, an outside day will close with prices higher and lower than the previous range with the close in the direction of the new trend.

Rules of Recognition

1. A definite trend must be underway.

2. The second day's body must completely engulf the prior day's body. This does not mean, however, that either the top or the bottom of the two bodies cannot be equal; it just means that both tops and both bottoms cannot be equal.

3. The first day's color should reflect the trend: black for a downtrend and white for an uptrend.

4. The second real body of the engulfing pattern should be the opposite color of the first real body.

Scenarios and Psychology Behind the Pattern

Bearish Engulfing Pattern

An uptrend is in place when a small white body day occurs with not much volume. The next day, prices open at new highs and then quickly sell off. The sell-off is sustained by high volume and finally closes below the open of the previous day. Emotionally, the uptrend has been damaged. If the next (third) day's prices remain lower, a major reversal of the uptrend has occurred.

A similar, but opposite, scenario would exist for the bullish Engulfing pattern.

Pattern Flexibility

The second day of the engulfing pattern engulfs more than the real body; in other words, if the second day engulfs the shadows of the first day, the success of the pattern will be much greater.

The color of the first day should reflect the trend of the market. In an uptrend, the first day should be white, and vice versa. The color of the second, or the engulfing day, should be the opposite of the first day.

Engulfing means that no part of the first day's real body is equal to or outside of the second day's real body. If the first day's real body was engulfed by at least 30 percent, a much stronger pattern exists.

Pattern Breakdown

Figure 3-6

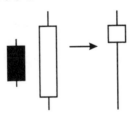

Figure 3-7

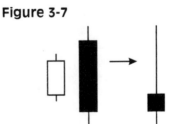

The bullish Engulfing pattern reduces to a Paper Umbrella or Hammer, which reflects a market turning point (Figure 3-6). The bearish Engulfing pattern reduces to a pattern similar to the Shooting Star or possibly a Gravestone Doji, if the body is very small (Figure 3-7). Both the bullish and bearish Engulfing patterns reduce to single lines that fully support their interpretation.

Related Patterns

The Engulfing pattern is also the first two days of the Three Outside patterns. The bullish Engulfing pattern would become the Three Outside Up pattern if the third day closed higher. Likewise, the bearish Engulfing pattern would make up the Three Outside Down pattern if the third day closed lower.

The Engulfing pattern is also a follow-through, or more advanced stage, of the Piercing Line and the Dark Cloud Cover. Because of this, the Engulfing pattern is considered more important.

Examples

Figure 3-8A

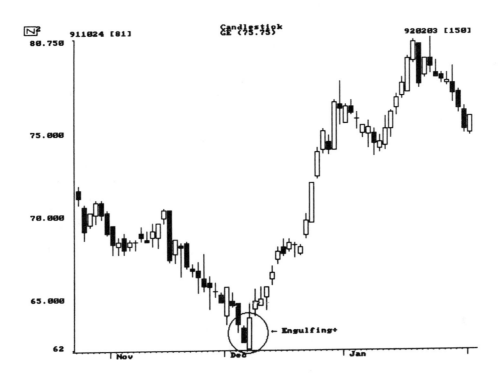

Figure 3-8B

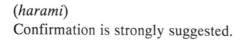

Harami

(*harami*)
Confirmation is strongly suggested.

Figure 3-9

Figure 3-10

Commentary

The Harami pattern is made up of the opposite arrangement of days as the Engulfing pattern (Figures 3-9 and 3-10). Harami is a Japanese word for pregnant or body within. You will find that in most instances the real bodies in the Harami are opposite in color, also like the Engulfing pattern.

You will probably note that the Harami is quite similar to the traditional inside day. The difference, of course, is that the traditional inside day uses the highs and lows, whereas the Harami is concerned only with the body (open and close). This requirement to use the open and close prices instead of the high and low prices is common in Japanese candlestick analysis and philosophy. The Harami requires that the body of the second day be completely engulfed by the body of the first day.

Rules of Recognition

1. A long day is preceded by a reasonable trend.

2. The color of the long first day is not as important, but it is best if it reflects the trend of the market.

3. A short day follows the long day, with its body completely inside the body range of the long day. Just like the Engulfing day, the tops or bottoms of the bodies can be equal, but both tops and both bottoms cannot be equal.

4. The short day should be the opposite color of the long day.

Scenarios and Psychology Behind the Pattern

Bullish Harami

A downtrend has been in place for some time. A long black day with average volume has occurred which helps to perpetuate the bearishness.

33

The next day, prices open higher, which shocks many complacent bears, and many shorts are quickly covered, causing the price to rise further. The price rise is tempered by the usual late comers seeing this as an opportunity to short the trend they missed the first time. Volume on this day has exceeded the previous day, which suggests strong short covering. A confirmation of the reversal on the third day would provide the needed proof that the trend has reversed.

Bearish Harami

An uptrend is in place and is perpetuated with a long white day and high volume. The next day, prices open lower and stay in a small range throughout the day, closing even lower, but still within the previous day's body. In view of this sudden deterioration of trend, traders should become concerned about the strength of this market, especially if volume is light. It certainly appears that the trend is about to change. Confirmation on the third day would be a lower close.

Pattern Flexibility

The long day should reflect the trend; in an uptrend the long day should be white and a downtrend should produce a black long day. The amount of engulfing of the second day by the first day should be significant. The long day should engulf the short day by at least 30 percent. Remember that long days are based upon the data preceding them.

Pattern Breakdown

Figure 3-11　　　　　　　　　　**Figure 3-12**

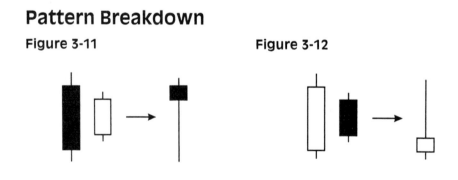

The bullish Harami reduces to a Paper Umbrella or a Hammer line which indicates a market turning point (Figure 3-11). The bearish Harami reduces to a Shooting Star line, which also is a bearish line (Figure 3-12). Both the bullish and the bearish Harami are supported by their single-line breakdowns.

Related Patterns

The Harami pattern is the first two days of the Three Inside Up and Three Inside Down patterns. A bullish Harami would be part of the Three Inside Up and a bearish Harami would be part of the Three Inside Down.

Examples

Figure 3-13A

Figure 3-13B

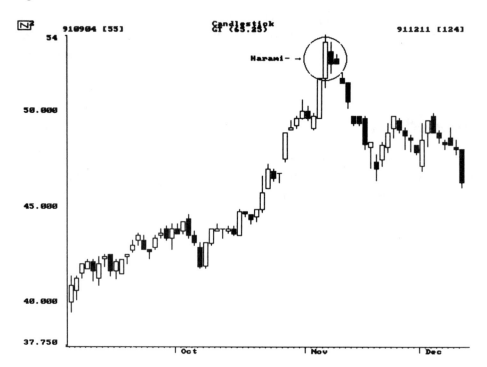

Harami Cross

(harami yose sen)
Confirmation is not required, but is recommended.

Figure 3-14   **Figure 3-15**

Commentary

The Harami pattern consists of a long body followed by a smaller body. It is the relative size of these two bodies that make the Harami important. Remember that Doji days, where the open and close price are equal, represent days of indecision. Therefore, small body days that occur after longer body days can also represent a day of indecision. The more the indecision and uncertainty, the more likelihood of a trend change. When the body of the second day becomes a Doji, the pattern is referred to as a Harami Cross (Figures 3-14 and 3-15), with the cross being the Doji. The Harami Cross is a better reversal pattern than the regular Harami.

Rules of Recognition

1. A long day occurs within a trending market.

2. The second day is a Doji (open and close are equal).

3. The second-day Doji is within the range of the previous long day.

Scenarios and Psychology Behind the Pattern

The psychology behind the Harami Cross starts out the same as that for the basic Harami pattern. A trend has been in place when, all of a sudden, the market gyrates throughout a day without exceeding the body range of the previous day. What's worse, the market closes at the same price as it opened. Volume of this Doji day also drys up, reflecting the complete lack of decision of traders. A significant reversal of trend has occurred.

Pattern Flexibility

The color of the long day should reflect the trend. The Doji can have an open and a close price that are within 2 to 3 percent of each other if, and only if, there are not many Doji days in the preceding data.

Pattern Breakdown

Figure 3-16   **Figure 3-17**

The bullish and bearish Harami Crosses reduce to single lines that support their interpretation in most instances (Figures 3-16 and 3-17). The body of the single-day reduction can be considerably longer than what is allowed for a Paper Umbrella or Hammer line. The fact that the breakdown is not contrary to the pattern is supportive.

Related Patterns

The Harami Cross could possibly be the beginning of a Rising or a Falling Three Methods, depending on the next few days' price action. The Rising and Falling Three Methods patterns are continuation patterns, which are in conflict with the signal given by the Harami Cross.

Examples

Figure 3-18A

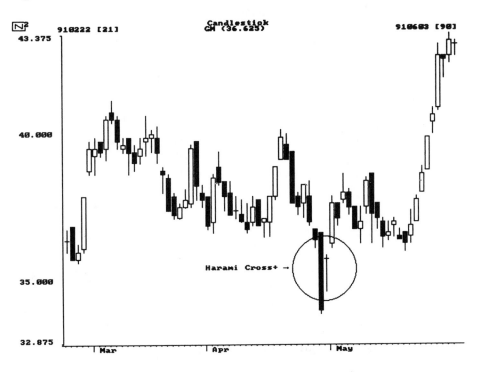

Figure 3-18B

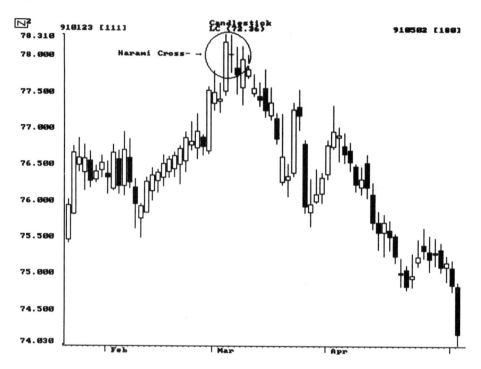

Inverted Hammer and Shooting Star

(*tohba* and *nagare boshi*)
Confirmation is definitely required.

Figure 3-19   **Figure 3-20**

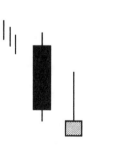

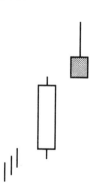

Commentary

Inverted Hammer

The Inverted Hammer is a bottom reversal line (Figure 3-19). Similar to its cousin the Hammer, it occurs in a downtrend and represents a possible reversal of trend. Common with most single and double candlestick patterns, it is important to wait for verification, in this case bullish verification. This could be in the form of the next day's opening above the Inverted Hammer's body. Since the closing price is near the low for the day and the market actually traded much higher, verification is most important. Additionally, there is little reference to this pattern in Japanese literature.

Shooting Star

The Shooting Star (Figure 3-20) is a single-line pattern that indicates an end to the upward move. It is not a major reversal signal. The Shooting Star line looks exactly the same as the Inverted Hammer. The difference, of course, is that the Shooting Star occurs at market tops. A rally attempt was completely aborted when the close occurred near the low of the day. The body of the Shooting Star does gap above the previous day's body. This fact actually means that the Shooting Star could be referred to as a two-line pattern since the previous day's body must be considered.

Rules of Recognition

Inverted Hammer

1. A small real body is formed near the lower part of the price range.

2. No gap down is required, as long as the pattern falls after a downtrend.

3. The upper shadow is usually no more than two times as long as the body.

4. The lower shadow is virtually nonexistent.

Shooting Star

1. Prices gap open after an uptrend.

2. A small real body is formed near the lower part of the price range.

3. The upper shadow is at least three times as long as the body.

4. The lower shadow is virtually nonexistent.

Scenario and Psychology Behind the Pattern

Inverted Hammer

A downtrend has been in place when the market opens with a down gap. A rally throughout the day fails to hold and the market closes near its low. Similar to the scenario of the Hammer and the Hanging Man, the opening of the following day is critical to the success or failure of this pattern to call a reversal of trend. If the next day opens above the Inverted Hammer's body, a potential trend reversal will cause shorts to be covered which would also perpetuate the rally. Similarly, an Inverted Hammer could easily become the middle day of a more bullish Morning Star pattern (page 56).

Shooting Star

During an uptrend, the market gaps open, rallies to a new high, and then closes near its low. This action, following a gap up, can only be considered as bearish. Certainly, it would cause some concern to any bulls who have profits.

Pattern Flexibility

Single-day candlesticks allow little flexibility. The length of the shadow will help in determining its strength. The upper shadow should be at least twice the length of the body. There should be no lower shadow, or at least not more than 5 to 10 percent of the high-low range. Like most situations, the color of the body can help, if it reflects the sentiment of the pattern.

Pattern Breakdown

Figure 3-21   **Figure 3-22**

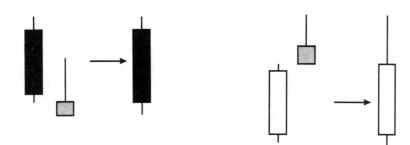

Even though the Inverted Hammer and the Shooting Star are considered as single-day patterns, the previous day must be used to add to the patterns' successfulness. The Inverted Hammer pattern reduces to a long black candle line, which is always viewed as a bearish indication when considered alone (Figure 3-21). The Shooting Star pattern reduces to a long white candle line, which almost always is considered a bullish line (Figure 3-22). Both of these patterns are in direct conflict with their breakdowns. This indicates that further confirmation should always be required before acting on them.

Related Patterns

As the Hammer and Hanging Man were related to the Dragonfly Doji, the Shooting Star and Inverted Hammer are cousins to the Gravestone Doji.

Examples

Figure 3-23A

Figure 3-23B

Piercing Line

(*kirikomi*)
Bullish reversal pattern.
Confirmation is suggested, but not required.

Figure 3-24

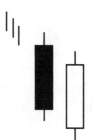

Commentary

The Piercing Line pattern, shown in Figure 3-24, is essentially the opposite of the Dark Cloud Cover (see next pattern). This pattern occurs in a downtrending market and is a two line or two day pattern. The first day is black which supports the downtrend and the second day is a long white day which opens at a new low and then closes above the midpoint of the preceding black day. *Kirikomi* means a cutback or a switchback.

Rules of Recognition

1. The first day is a long black body continuing the downtrend.

2. The second day is a white body which opens below the low of the previous day (that's low, not close).

3. The second day closes within but above the midpoint of the previous day's body.

Scenarios and Psychology Behind the Pattern

A long black body forms in a downtrend which maintains the bearishness. A gap to the downside on the next day's open further perpetuates the bearishness. However, the market rallies all day and closes much higher. In fact the close is above the midpoint of the body of the long black day. This action causes concern to the bears and a potential bottom has been made. Candlestick charting shows this action quite well, where standard bar charting would hardly discern it.

Pattern Flexibility

The white real body should close more than halfway into the prior black candlestick's body. If it didn't, you probably should wait for more bullish confirmation. There is no flexibility to this rule with the Piercing pattern. The Piercing pattern's white candlestick must rise more than halfway into the black candlestick's body. There are three additional candle patterns called On Neck Line, In Neck Line, and Thrusting Line (covered in Chapter 4), which make the definition of the Piercing Line so stringent. These three patterns are similar to the Piercing Line but are classified as bearish continuation patterns since the second day doesn't rally nearly as much.

The more penetration into the prior day's black body, the more likely it will be a successful reversal pattern. Remember that if it closes above the body of the previous day, it is not a Piercing pattern, but a bullish Engulfing day.

Both days of the Piercing pattern should be long days. The second day must close above the midpoint and below the open of the first day, with no exceptions.

Pattern Breakdown

Figure 3-25

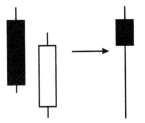

The Piercing Line pattern reduces to a Paper Umbrella or Hammer line, which is indicative of a market reversal or turning point (Figure 3-25). The single candle line reduction fully supports the bullishness of the Piercing Line.

Related Patterns

Three patterns begin in the same way as the Piercing Line. However, they do not quite give the reversal signal that the Piercing Line does and are considered continuation patterns. These are the On Neck Line, In Neck

Line, and Thrusting Line (see Chapter 4). The bullish Engulfing pattern is also an extension, or more mature situation, of the Piercing Line.

Example

Figure 3-26

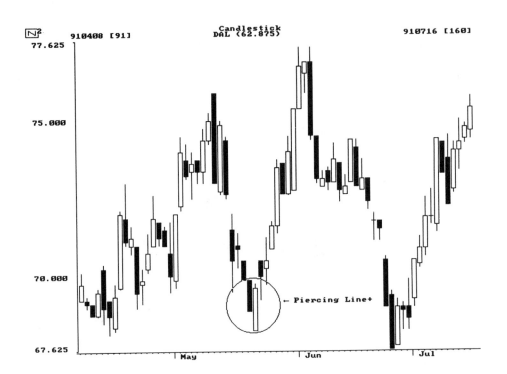

Dark Cloud Cover

(*kabuse*)
Bearish reversal pattern.
No confirmation is required.

Figure 3-27

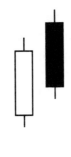

Commentary

The Dark Cloud Cover (Figure 3-27) is a bearish reversal pattern and the counterpart of the Piercing pattern (Figure 3-24). Since this pattern only occurs in an uptrend, the first day is a long white day which supports the trend. The second day opens above the high of the white day. This is one of the few times that the high or low is used in candle pattern definitions. Trading lower throughout the day results in the close being below the midpoint of the long white day.

This reversal pattern, like the opposite Piercing Line, has a marked affect on the attitude of traders because of the higher open followed by the much lower close. There are no exceptions to this pattern. *Kabuse* means to get covered or to hang over.

Rules of Recognition

1. The first day is a long white body which is continuing the uptrend.

2. The second day is a black body day with the open above the previous day's high (that's the high, not the close).

3. The second (black) day closes within and below the midpoint of the previous white body.

Scenarios and Psychology Behind the Pattern

The market is in an uptrend. Typical in an uptrend, a long white candlestick is formed. The next day the market gaps higher on the opening, however, that is all that is remaining to the uptrend. The market drops to close well into the body of the white day, in fact, below its midpoint. Anyone who was bullish would certainly have to rethink their strategy with this type of action. Like the Piercing Line, a significant reversal of trend has occurred.

Pattern Flexibility

The more penetration of the black body's close into the prior white body, the greater the chance for a top reversal. The first day should be a long day, with the second day opening significantly higher. This merely accentuates the reversal of sentiment in the market.

Pattern Breakdown

Figure 3-28

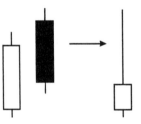

The Dark Cloud Cover pattern reduces to a Shooting Star line, which supports the bearishness of the pattern (Figure 3-28). If the second day's black body closes deeply into the first day, the breakdown would be a Gravestone Doji, which also fully supports the bearishness.

Related Patterns

The Dark Cloud Cover is also the beginning of a bearish Engulfing pattern. Because of this, it would make the bearish Engulfing pattern a more bearish reversal signal than the Dark Cloud Cover.

Example

Figure 3-29

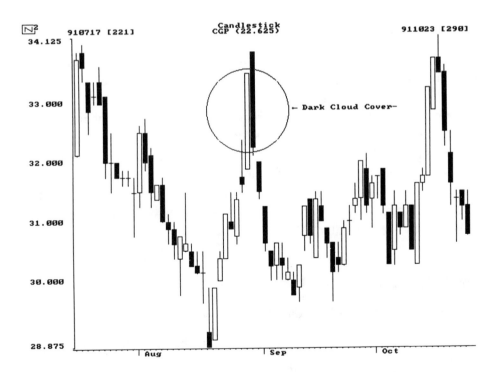

Doji Star

(doji bike)
Confirmation is suggested.

Figure 3-30

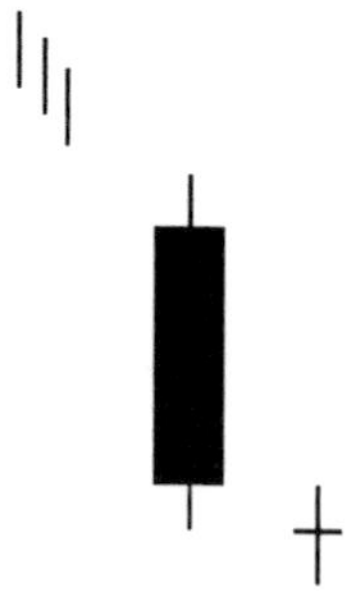

Figure 3-31

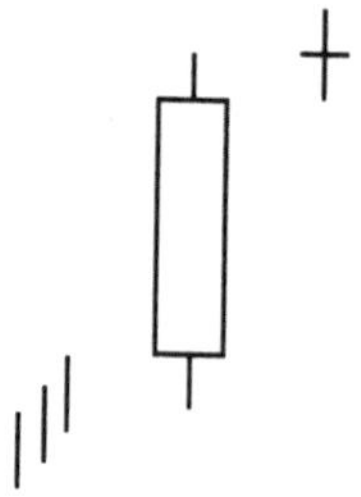

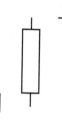

Commentary

A Doji Star is a warning that a trend is about to change. It is a long real body which should reflect the previous trend. A downtrend should produce a black body, an uptrend, a white body (Figures 3-30 and 3-31). The next day, prices gap in the direction of trend, then close at the opening. This deterioration of the previous trend is immediate cause for concern. The clear message of the Doji Star is an excellent example of the value of the candlestick method of charting. If you were using close only or standard bar charts, the deterioration of the trend would not quite yet be apparent. Candlesticks, however, show that the trend is abating because of the gap in real bodies by the Doji Star.

Rules of Recognition

1. The first day is a long day.

2. The second day gaps in the direction of the previous trend.

3. The second day is a Doji.

4. The shadows on the Doji day should not be excessively long, especially in the bullish case.

Scenarios and Psychology Behind the Pattern

Considering the bearish Doji Star, the market is in an uptrend and is further confirmed by a strong white day. The next day gaps even higher, trades in a small range, and then closes at or near its open. This will erode almost all confidence from the previous rally. Many positions have been changed, which caused the Doji in the first place. The next day's open, if lower, would set the stage for a reversal of trend.

Pattern Flexibility

If the gap can also contain the shadows, the significance of the trend change is greater. The first day should also reflect the trend with its body color.

Pattern Breakdown

Figure 3-32   **Figure 3-33**

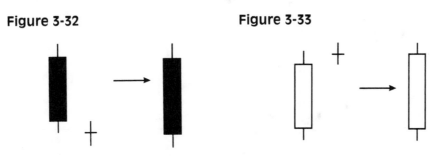

The bullish Doji Star reduces to a long black candlestick, which does not support the bullishness of the pattern (Figure 3-32). The bearish Doji Star reduces to a long white candle line, which puts it in direct conflict with the pattern (Figure 3-33). These breakdown conflicts should not be ignored.

Related Patterns

The Doji Star is the first two days of either the Morning or Evening Doji Star.

Examples

Figure 3-34A

Figure 3-34B

Morning Star and Evening Star

(*sankawa ake no myojyo* and *sankawa yoi no myojyo*)
No confirmation is required.

Figure 3-35   **Figure 3-36**

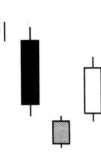 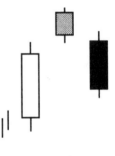

Commentary

Morning Star

The Morning Star is a bullish reversal pattern. Its name indicates that it foresees higher prices. It is made of a long black body followed by a small body which gaps lower (Figure 3-35). The third day is a white body that moves into the first day's black body. An ideal Morning Star would have a gap before and after the middle (star) day's body.

Evening Star

The bearish counterpart of the Morning Star is the Evening Star. Since the Evening Star is a bearish pattern, it appears after, or during, an uptrend. The first day is a long white body followed by a star (Figure 3-36). Remember that a star's body gaps away from the previous day's body. The star's smaller body is the first sign of indecision. The third day gaps down and closes even lower completing this pattern. Like the Morning Star, the Evening Star should have a gap between the first and second bodies and then another gap between the second and third bodies. Some literature does not refer to the second gap.

Rules of Recognition

1. The first day is always the color that was established by the ensuing trend. That is, an uptrend will yield a long white day for the first day of the Evening Star and a downtrend will yield a black first day of the Morning Star.

2. The second day, the star, is always gapped from the body of the first day. It's color is not important.

3. The third day is always the opposite color of the first day.

4. The first day, and most likely the third day, are considered long days.

Scenarios and Psychology Behind the Pattern

Morning Star

A downtrend has been in place which is assisted by a long black candlestick. There is little doubt about the downtrend continuing with this type of action. The next day prices gap lower on the open, trade within a small range and close near their open. This small body shows the beginning of indecision. The next day prices gap higher on the open and then close much higher. A significant reversal of trend has occurred.

Evening Star

The scenario of the Evening Star is the exact opposite of the Morning Star.

Pattern Flexibility

Ideally there is one gap between the bodies of the first candlestick and the star, and a second gap between the bodies of the star and the third candlestick. Some flexibility is possible in the gap between the star and the third day.

If the third candlestick closes deeply into the first candlestick's real body, a much stronger move should ensue, especially if heavy volume occurs on the third day. Some literature likes to see the third day close more than halfway into the body of the first day.

Pattern Breakdown

Figure 3-37   **Figure 3-38**

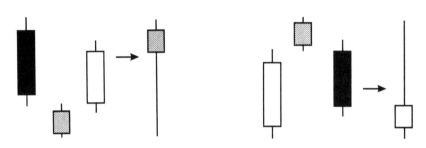

The Morning Star reduces to a Paper Umbrella or Hammer line, which fully supports the Morning Star's bullish indication (Figure 3-37). The Evening Star pattern reduces to a Shooting Star line, which is also a bearish line and in full support (Figure 3-38).

Related Patterns

The next few patterns are all specific versions of the Morning and Evening Stars. They are the Morning and Evening Doji Stars, the Abandoned Baby, and the Tri Star.

Examples

Figure 3-39A

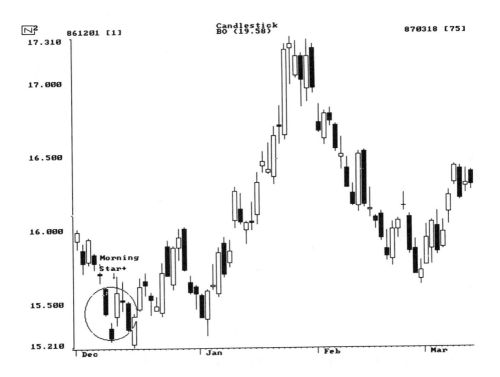

Figure 3-39B

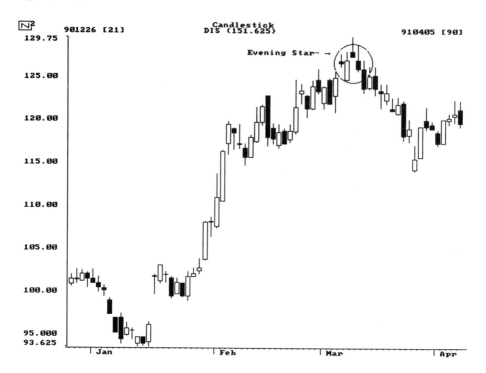

The Morning and Evening Doji Stars

(*ake no myojyo doji bike* and *yoi no myojyo doji bike minami jyuji sei*)
No confirmation is required.

Figure 3-40   **Figure 3-41**

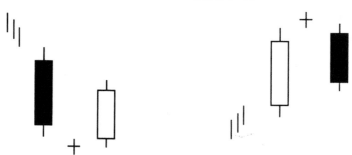

Commentary

Remember from the discussion of the Doji Star that a possible reversal of trend is occurring because of the indecision associated with the Doji. Doji Stars are warnings that the prior trend is probably going to at least change. The day after the Doji should confirm the impending trend reversal. The Morning and Evening Doji Star patterns do exactly this.

Morning Doji Star

A downtrending market is in place with a long black candlestick which is followed by a Doji Star. Just like the regular Morning Star, confirmation on the third day fully supports the reversal of trend. This type of Morning Star, the Morning Doji Star (Figure 3-40), can represent a significant reversal. It is therefore considered more significant than the regular Morning Star pattern.

Evening Doji Star

A Doji Star in an uptrend followed by a long black body that closed well into the first day's white body would confirm a top reversal (Figure 3-41). The regular Evening Star pattern has a small body as its star, whereas the Evening Doji Star has a Doji as its star. The Evening Doji Star is more important because of this Doji. The Evening Doji Star has also been referred to as the Southern Cross.

Rules of Recognition

1. Like many reversal patterns, the first day's color should represent the trend of the market.

2. The second day must be a Doji Star (a Doji that gaps).

3. The third day is the opposite color of the first day.

Scenarios and Psychology Behind the Pattern

The psychology behind these patterns is similar to those of the regular Morning and Evening Star patterns, except that the Doji Star is more of a shock to the previous trend and, therefore, more significant.

Pattern Flexibility

Flexibility may occur in the amount of penetration into the first day's body by the third day. If penetration is greater than 50 percent, this pattern has a better chance to be successful.

Pattern Breakdown

Figure 3-42

Figure 3-43

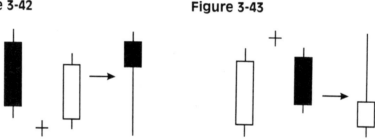

The Morning Doji Star reduces to a Hammer pattern (Figure 3-42) and on occasion will reduce to a Dragonfly Doji line. The Evening Doji Star reduces to a Shooting Star line (Figure 3-43) and occasionally to a Gravestone Doji line. The closer the breakdown is to the single Doji lines, the greater the support for the pattern, because the third day closes further into the body of the first day.

Related Patterns

You should be aware that this pattern starts with the Doji Star. It is the confirmation that is needed with the Doji Star and should not be ignored.

Examples

Figure 3-44A

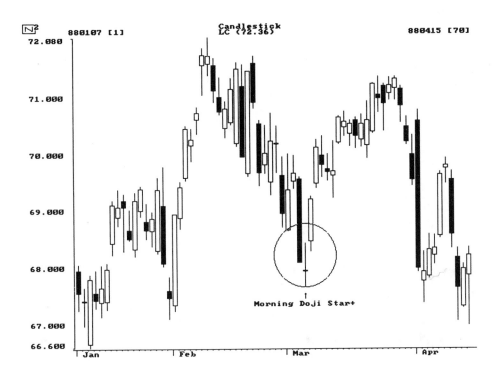

Morning Doji Star+

Figure 3-44B

Abandoned Baby

(*sute go*)
No confirmation is required.

Figure 3-45   **Figure 3-46**

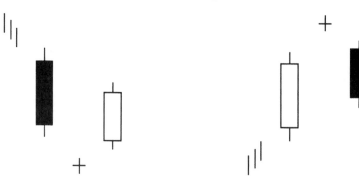

Commentary

Another major reversal pattern that is similar in format to the family of Morning and Evening Star patterns is the Abandoned Baby pattern. This pattern is almost exactly the same as the Morning and Evening Doji Star pattern with one important exception. Here, the shadows on the Doji must also gap below the shadows of the first and third days for the Abandoned Baby bottom (Figure 3-45). The opposite is true for the Abandoned Baby top (Figure 3-46), the Doji must completely (including shadows) gap above the surrounding days. The Abandoned Baby is quite rare.

Rules of Recognition

1. The first day should reflect the prior trend.

2. The second day is a Doji whose shadows gap above or below the previous day's upper or lower shadow.

3. The third day is the opposite color of the first day.

4. The third day gaps in the opposite direction with no shadows overlapping.

Scenarios and Psychology Behind the Pattern

Like most of the three day star patterns, the scenarios are similar. The primary difference is that the star (second day) can reflect greater deterioration in the prior trend, depending on whether it gaps, is Doji, and so on.

Pattern Flexibility

Because of the specific parameters used to define this pattern, there is not much room for flexibility. This is a special case of the Morning and Evening Doji Stars in which the second day is similar to a traditional island reversal day.

Pattern Breakdown

Figure 3-47   **Figure 3-48**

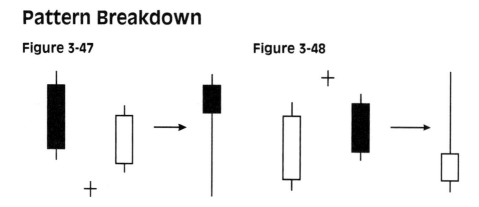

The breakdown of the Abandoned Baby patterns, both bullish and bearish, are extensions of the Morning and Evening Doji Stars (Figures 3-47 and 3-48). The bullishness or bearishness is further amplified because the long shadow is usually longer than in the previous cases. As before, the more that the third day closes into the first day's body, the closer these breakdowns are to the Dragonfly and Gravestone Doji lines.

Related Patterns

This is a special case of the Doji Star in that the Doji day gaps from the previous day. This gap includes all shadows, not just the body. The third day gaps also, but in the opposite direction.

Examples

Figure 3-49A

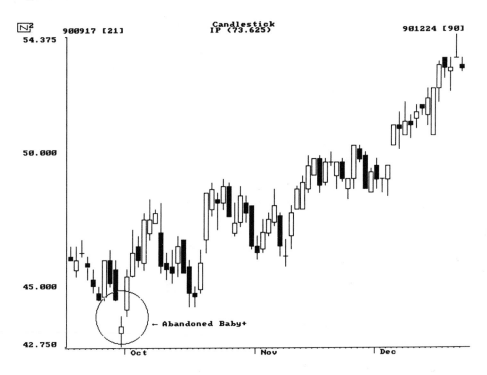

Figure 3-49B

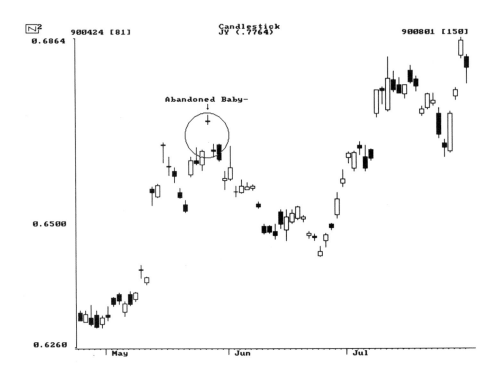

The Tri Star

(*santen boshi*)
Confirmation is suggested.

Figure 3-50   **Figure 3-51**

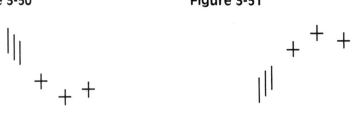

Commentary

The Tri Star pattern (Figures 3-50 and 3-51) was developed by Steve Nison. It is made up of three Doji days with the middle Doji day being a star. This pattern is extremely rare, but when it occurs should not be ignored.

Rules of Recognition

1. All three days are Doji.

2. The second day gaps above or below the first and third day.

Scenarios and Psychology Behind the Pattern

The market has probably been in an uptrend or downtrend for a long time. With the trend starting to show weakness, bodies probably are becoming smaller. The first Doji would cause considerable concern. The second Doji would indicate that there was no direction left in the market. And finally, the third Doji would put the final nail in the coffin of this trend. Because this indicates entirely too much indecision, everyone with any conviction would be reversing positions.

Pattern Flexibility

Be careful with this one. Because the Tri Star is so rare, you should probably be suspect of the data used in its calculation. If the middle Doji gap includes the shadows, it would be even more significant.

Pattern Breakdown

Figure 3-52   **Figure 3-53**

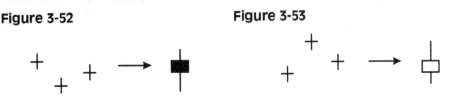

The Tri Star patterns break down into Spinning Tops which are indicative of market indecision (Figures 3-52 and 3-53). This is somewhat of a conflict with the Tri Star pattern and supports the notion that because this pattern is so rare, it should be viewed with some skepticism.

Related Patterns

Based on the previous discussions, you can see what a rare pattern this is.

Examples

Figure 3-54A

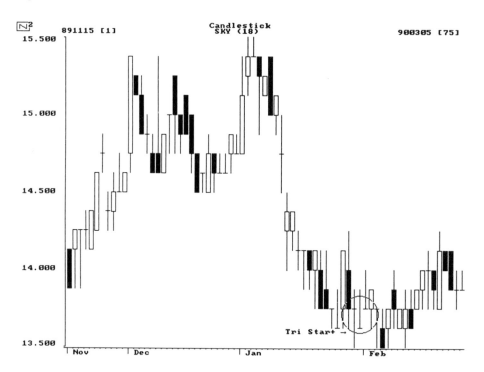

Figure 3-54B

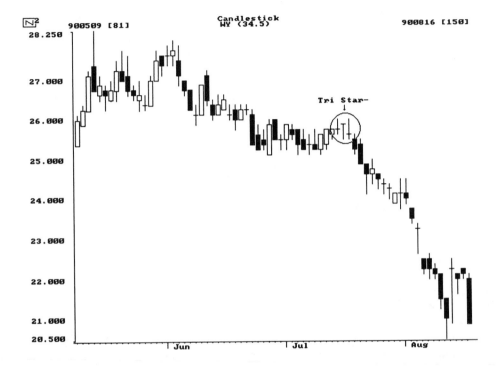

Upside Gap Two Crows

(*shita banare niwa garasu*)
Bearish reversal pattern.
Confirmation is not required, but is mildly suggested.

Figure 3-55

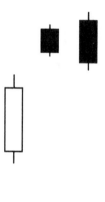

Commentary

This pattern only occurs in an uptrend. As with most bearish reversal patterns, it begins with a white body candlestick. The gap referred to in the name of this pattern is the gap between, not only the first and second days, but also the first and third days. The second and third days are black which is where the two crows originate.

The third day (second black day) should open higher and then close lower than the close of the second day. The third day, even though closing lower than the second day, still is gapped above the first day. Simply said, the second black day engulfs the first black day.

Rules of Recognition

1. An uptrend continues with a long white day.

2. An upward gapping black day is formed after the white day.

3. A second black day opens above the first black day and closes below the body of the first black day. Its body engulfs the first black day.

4. The close of the second black day is still above the close of the long white day.

Scenarios and Psychology Behind the Pattern

Like the beginning of most bearish reversal patterns a white body day occurs in an uptrend. The next day opens with a higher gap, fails to rally and closes lower forming a black day. This is not too worrisome because it still did not get lower than the first day's close. On the third day prices again gap to a higher open and then drop to close lower than the previous day's close. This closing price, however, is still above the close of the white first day. The bullishness is bound to subside. How can you have two successively lower closes and still be a raging bull?

Pattern Flexibility

The Upside Gap Two Crows pattern is fairly rigid. If the third day (second black day) were to close into the white day's body, the pattern would become a Two Crows pattern (discussed later in this chapter).

Pattern Breakdown

Figure 3-56

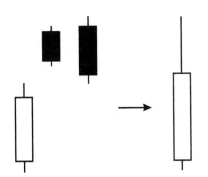

The Upside Gap Two Crows pattern reduces to a candle line whose white body is slightly longer than the first day's white body and has a long upper shadow (Figure 3-56). The fact that this is not exactly a bearish candle line suggests that some further confirmation is required before acting on this pattern.

Related Patterns

A failure of the third day's black body to open slightly below the second day's open and remain above the first day's body could lead to this pattern's becoming a Mat Hold continuation pattern. The Mat Hold is a bullish continuation pattern discussed in the next chapter. Also, the first two days of this pattern could become an Evening Star, depending upon what happens the third day.

Example

Figure 3-57

Meeting Lines

(deai sen or *gyakushu sen)*
Confirmation is suggested.

Figure 3-58

Figure 3-59

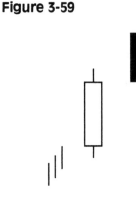

Commentary

Meeting Lines are formed when opposite-colored candlesticks have the same closing price. Some literature refers to Meeting Lines as Counterattack Lines. *Deaisen* means lines that meet and *gyakushusen* means counteroffensive lines.

Bullish Meeting Line

This pattern normally occurs during a decline. The first day of this pattern is a long black candlestick (Figure 3-58). The next day opens sharply lower and puts the downtrend into a promising position. The bullish Meeting Line is somewhat similar in concept to the bullish Piercing Line, with the difference being the amount the second day rebounds. The Meeting Line only rises up to the first day's close while the Piercing Line's second day goes above the midpoint of the first day's body. The bullish Meeting Line is not as significant at the Piercing Line. Also, do not confuse this with the On Neck Line covered in Chapter 4.

Bearish Meeting Line

An almost opposite relationship exists for the bearish Meeting Line relative to the Dark Cloud Cover. The bearish Meeting Line (Figure 3-59) opens at a new high and then closes at the same close of the previous day, while the Dark Cloud cover drops to below the midpoint.

Rules of Recognition

1. Two lines have bodies that extend the current trend.

2. The first body's color always reflects the trend: black for downtrends and white for uptrends.

3. The second body is the opposite color.

4. The close of each day is the same.

5. Both days should be long days.

Scenarios and Psychology Behind the Pattern

Bullish Meeting Line

The market has been in a downtrend when a long black day forms, which further perpetuates the trend. The next day opens with a gap down, then rallies throughout the day to close at the same close as the previous day. This fact shows how previous price benchmarks are used by traders: the odds are very good that a reversal has taken place. If the third day opens higher, confirmation has been given.

Pattern Flexibility

The Meeting Line pattern should consist of two long lines. However, many times the second day is not nearly as long as the first day. This doesn't seem to affect the pattern's ability; confirmation is still suggested. It is also best if each day is a Closing Marubozu.

Pattern Breakdown

Figure 3-60   **Figure 3-61**

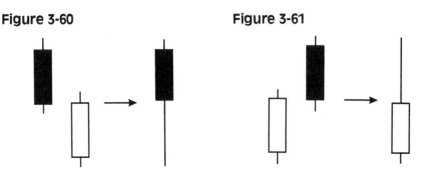

The Meeting Lines break down into single candle lines that offer no support for their case (Figure 3-60 and 3-61). The single lines are similar to the first line in the pattern, with a shadow that extends in the direction of the second day. Again, the breakdown neither confirms the pattern nor indicates lack of support.

Related Patterns

Somewhat opposite in appearance are the Separating Lines, which are continuation patterns. One can also see the potential for these lines to become a Dark Cloud Cover or a Piercing Line, if there is any penetration of the first body by the second.

Examples

Figure 3-62A

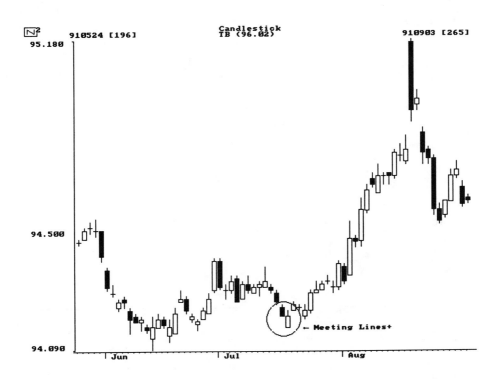

Figure 3-62B

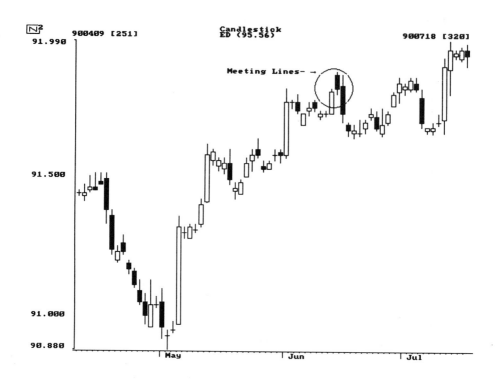

Belt Hold

(*yorikiri*)
Confirmation is required.

Figure 3-63

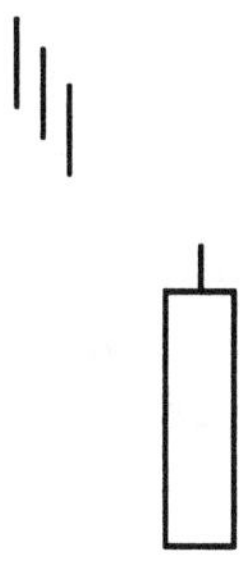

Figure 3-64

Commentary

Belt Hold lines are also opening marubozu lines (Chapter 2). Remember that the opening marubozu does not have a shadow extending from the open end of the body. The bullish Belt Hold (Figure 3-63) is a white opening marubozu that occurs in a downtrend. It opens on the low of the day, rallies significantly against the previous trend, and then closes near its high but not necessarily at its high. The bearish Belt Hold (Figure 3-64) is a black opening marubozu that occurs in an uptrend. Similarly, it opens on its high, trades against the trend of the market, and then closes near its low. Longer bodies for Belt Hold lines will offer more resistance to the trend that they are countering.

Belt Hold lines, like most of the single day patterns lose their importance if there are many of them in close proximity. The Japanese name of *yorikiri* means to push out. Steve Nison coined the name of Belt Hold.

Rules of Recognition

1. The Belt Hold line is identified by the lack of a shadow on one end.

2. The bullish white Belt Hold opens on its low and has no lower shadow.

3. The bearish black Belt Hold opens on its high and has no upper shadow.

Scenarios and Psychology Behind the Pattern

The market is trending when a significant gap in the direction of trend occurs on the open. From that point, the market never looks back: all further price action that day is the opposite of the previous trend. This causes much concern and many positions will be covered or sold, which will help accentuate the reversal.

Pattern Flexibility

Since this is single candle line pattern, there is not much room for any flexibility. It should be a long day. Remember, a day is considered long in relation to the previous few days only.

Pattern Breakdown

Single candle line patterns cannot be reduced further.

Related Patterns

The Belt Hold pattern is the same as the Opening Marubozu, discussed in Chapter 2. Like the Marubozu, the Belt Hold will form the first day of many more advanced candle patterns.

Examples

Figure 3-65A

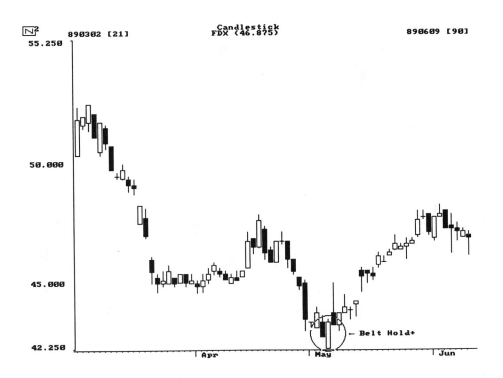

Figure 3-65B

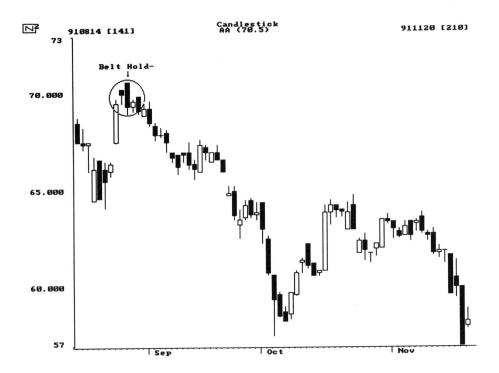

Unique Three River Bottom

(*sankawa soko zukae*)
Bullish reversal pattern.
Confirmation is not required, but is suggested.

Figure 3-66

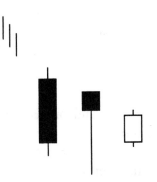

Commentary

As demonstrated by Figure 3-66, the Unique Three River Bottom is a pattern somewhat like a Morning Star. The trend is down and a long black real body is formed. The next day opens higher, trades at a new low, then closes near the high, producing a small black body. The third day opens lower, but not lower than the low that was made on the second day. A small white body is formed on the third day, which closes below the close of the second day. The Unique Three River Bottom is extremely rare.

Rules of Recognition

1. The first day is a long black day.

2. The second day is a Harami day, but the body is also black.

3. The second day has a lower shadow that sets a new low.

4. The third day is a short white day which is below the middle day.

Scenarios and Psychology Behind the Pattern

A falling market produces a long black day. The next day opens higher, but the bearish strength causes a new low to be set. A substantial rally ensues in which the strength of the bears is in question. This indecision and lack of stability is enforced when the third day opens lower. Stability arrives with a small white body on the third day. If, on the fourth day, price rises to new highs, a reversal of trend has been confirmed.

Pattern Flexibility

Because this is such an unusual and precise pattern, there is not much flexibility. If the lower shadow on the second day were quite long, the greater potential for reversal would be more likely. In some literature, the second day resembles a Hammer line. Like many reversal patterns, if volume supports the reversal, the success is likely to be greater.

Pattern Breakdown

Figure 3-67

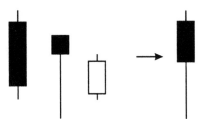

The Unique Three River Bottom pattern reduces to a single line that most likely is a Hammer line (Figure 3-67). The lower shadow must be at least twice as long as the body to be a Hammer, which, in this case, is quite possible because of the long lower shadow on the second day. The Hammer fully supports the bullishness of the Unique Three River Bottom pattern.

Related Patterns

This pattern is a take-off of the Morning Star, but doesn't look anything like it. Its appearance in Japanese literature is part of the Sakata Method (see Chapter 5).

Example

Figure 3-68

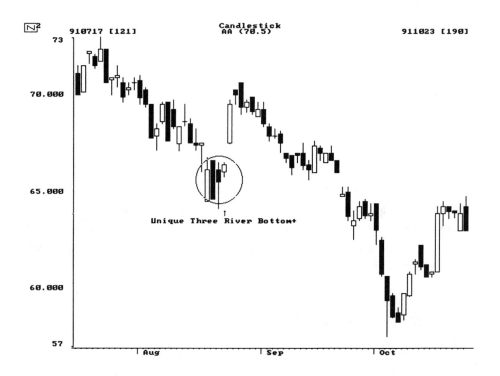

Three White Soldiers

(*aka sanpei*)
Bullish reversal pattern.
No confirmation is required.

Figure 3-69

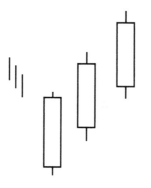

Commentary

The Three White Soldiers pattern is a vital part of the Sakata Method described in Chapter 5. It shows a series of long white candlesticks which progressively close at higher prices. It is also best if prices open in the middle of the previous day's range (body). This stair-step action is quite bullish and shows the downtrend has abruptly ended.

Rules of Recognition

1. Three consecutive long white lines occur, each with a higher close.

2. Each should open within the previous body.

3. Each should close at or near the high for the day.

Scenarios and Psychology Behind the Pattern

The Three White Soldiers pattern occurs in a downtrend and is representative of a strong reversal in the market. Each day opens lower but then closes to a new short term high. This type of price action is very bullish and should never be ignored.

Pattern Flexibility

The opening prices of the second and third days can be anywhere within the previous body. However, it is better to see the open above the midpoint of the previous day's body. Keep in mind that when a day opens for trading, some selling has to exist to open below the previous close. This suggests that a healthy rise is always accompanied by some selling.

Pattern Breakdown

Figure 3-70

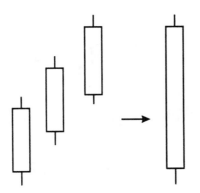

The Three White Soldiers pattern reduces to a very bullish long white candle line (Figure 3-70). This breakdown is in full support of the pattern, which makes confirmation unnecessary.

Related Patterns

See the next two patterns, Advance Block and Deliberation.

Examples

Figure 3-71

Advance Block

(*saki zumari*)
Bearish reversal pattern.
Confirmation is suggested.

Figure 3-72

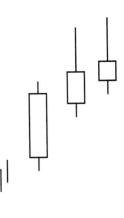

Commentary

As shown in Figure 3-72, this pattern is a derivation of the Three White Soldiers pattern. However, it must occur in an uptrend, whereas the Three White Soldiers must occur in a downtrend. Unlike the Three White Soldiers pattern, the second and third days of the Advance Block pattern show weakness. The long upper shadows show that the price extremes reached during the day cannot hold. This type of action after an uptrend and then for two days in a row should make any bullish market participants nervous, especially if the uptrend was getting overextended.

Remember, that this pattern occurs in an uptrend. Most multiple-day patterns begin with a long day, which helps support the existing trend. The two days with long upper shadows show that there is profit taking because the rise is losing its power.

Rules of Recognition

1. Three white days occur with consecutively higher closes.

2. Each day opens within the previous day's body.

3. A definite deterioration in the upward strength is evidenced by long upper shadows on the second and third days.

Scenarios and Psychology Behind the Pattern

The scenario of the Advance Block pattern closely resembles the events that could take place with the Three White Soldiers pattern. This situation, however, does not materialize into a strong advance. Rather, it weakens after the first day because the close is significantly lower than the high. The third day is as weak as the second day. Remember, weakness in this context is relative to the Three White Soldiers pattern.

Pattern Flexibility

Defining deterioration is difficult. Although this pattern starts out like the Three White Soldiers, it doesn't produce the upward strength and each day shows smaller body length and longer shadows. The second and third day need to trade higher than their closes.

Pattern Breakdown

Figure 3-73

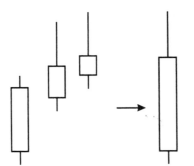

The Advance Block pattern reduces to a long white candle line that is not quite as long as the Three White Soldiers breakdown (Figure 3-73). This long white candlestick also has a long upper shadow, which shows that the prices did not close nearly as high as they got during the trading days. Because of this, the Advance Block is viewed as a bearish pattern. In most cases, this could only mean that long positions should be protected.

Related Patterns

This is a variation of the Three White Soldiers (discussed previously) and the Deliberation pattern (explored next).

Examples

Figure 3-74

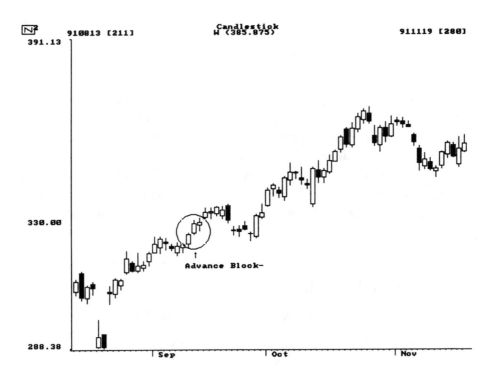

Deliberation

(aka sansei shian boshi)
Bearish reversal pattern.
Confirmation is suggested.

Figure 3-75

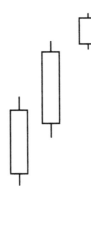

Commentary

As illustrated in Figure 3-75, the Deliberation pattern is also a derivative of the Three White Soldiers pattern. The first two long white candlesticks make a new high and are followed by a small white candlestick or a star. This pattern is also called a Stalled pattern in some literature. It is best if the last day gaps above the second day. Being a small body, this shows the indecision necessary to arrest the upmove. This indecision is the time of deliberation. A further confirmation could easily turn this pattern into an Evening Star pattern.

Rules of Recognition

1. The first and second day have long white bodies.

2. The third day opens near the second day's close.

3. The third day is a Spinning Top and most probably a star.

Scenarios and Psychology Behind the Pattern

This pattern exhibits a weakness similar to the Advance Block pattern in that it gets weak in a short period of time. The difference is that the weakness occurs all at once on the third day. The Deliberation pattern occurs after a sustained upward move and shows that trends cannot last forever. As with the Advance Block, defining the deterioration of the trend can be difficult.

Pattern Flexibility

If the third white body is also a star, watch for the next day to generate a possible Evening Star pattern.

Pattern Breakdown

Figure 3-76

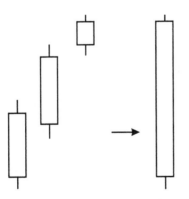

The Deliberation pattern reduces to a long white candlestick (Figure 3-76). This is in direct conflict with the pattern itself which suggest the need for further confirmation. A gap down on the following day would produce an Evening Star and therefore support this pattern's bearishness.

Related Patterns

See the previous two patterns, the Three White Soldiers and Advance Block.

Example

Figure 3-77

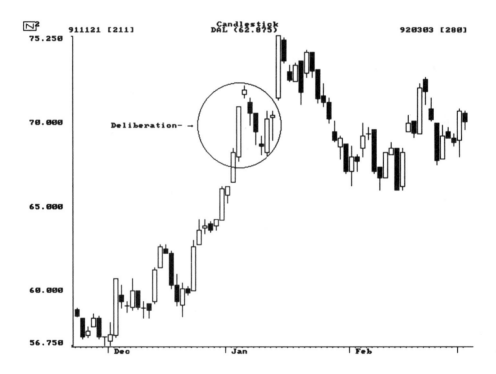

Three Black Crows

(*sanba garasu*)
Bearish reversal pattern.
No confirmation is required.

Figure 3-78

Commentary

The Three Black Crows is the counterpart of the Three White Soldiers pattern. Occurring during an uptrend, three long black days are stairstepping downward. "Bad news has wings," an old Japanese expression, easily fits this pattern. Each day opens slightly higher than the previous day's close, but then drops to a new closing low. When this occurs three times, a clear message of trend reversal has been sent. Be careful that this downward progression does not get overextended, that would surely cause some bottom picking from the eternal bulls.

Rules of Recognition

1. Three consecutive long black days occur.

2. Each day closes at a new low.

3. Each day opens within the body of the previous day.

4. Each day closes at or near its lows.

Scenarios and Psychology Behind the Pattern

The market is either approaching a top or has been at a high level for some time. A decisive trend move to the downside is made with a long black day. The next two days are accompanied by further erosion in prices caused by much selling and profit taking. This type of price action has to take its toll on the bullish mentality.

Pattern Flexibility

It would be good to see the real body of the first candlestick of the Three Black Crows under the prior white day's high. This would accelerate the bearishness of this pattern.

Pattern Breakdown

Figure 3-79

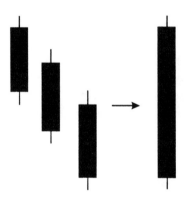

The Three Black Crows pattern reduces to a long black candlestick, which fully supports this pattern's bearishness (Figure 3-79).

Related Patterns

A more rigid version of this pattern is the Identical Three Crows (see the following pattern).

Example

Figure 3-80

Identical Three Crows

(*doji sanba garasu*)
Bearish reversal pattern.
No confirmation is required.

Figure 3-81

Commentary

This is a special case of the Three Black Crows pattern discussed earlier. The difference is that the second and third black days open at or near the previous day's close (Figure 3-81).

Rules of Recognition

1. Three long black days are stair-stepping downward.

2. Each day starts at the previous day's close.

Scenarios and Psychology Behind the Pattern

This pattern resembles a panic selling that should cause additional downside action. Each day's close sets a benchmark for opening prices the next trading day. There is a total absence of buying power in this pattern.

Pattern Flexibility

Because this pattern is a special version of the Three Black Crows pattern, flexibility is almost nonexistent.

Pattern Breakdown

Figure 3-82

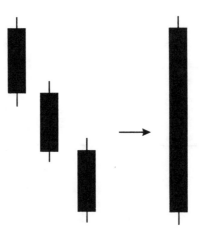

Like the Three Black Crows pattern, the Identical Three Crows reduces to a long black candlestick (Figure 3-82). This fully supports the pattern's bearish implications.

Related Patterns

This is a variation of the Three Black Crows pattern.

Example

Figure 3-83

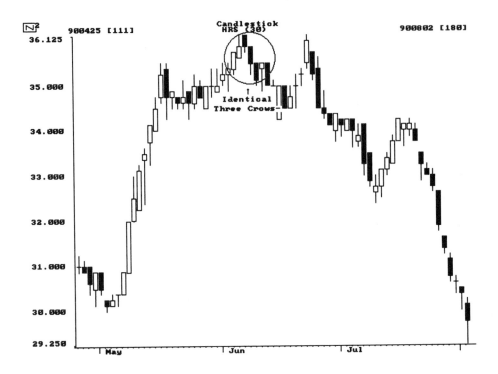

Breakaway

(hanare sante no shinte zukae)
Confirmation is recommended, especially for the bearish Breakaway pattern.

Figure 3-84   **Figure 3-85**

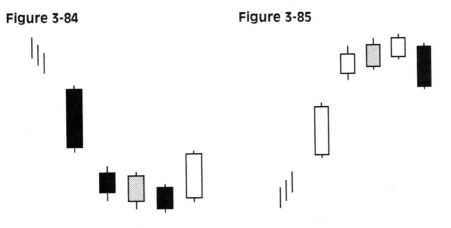

Commentary

Bullish Breakaway

The bullish Breakaway pattern comes during a downtrend and represents an acceleration of selling to a possible oversold position. The pattern starts with a long black day followed by another black day whose body gaps down (Figure 3-84). After the down gap, the next three days set consecutively lower prices. All days in this pattern are black, with the exception of the third day, which may be either black or white. The three days after the gap are similar to the Three Black Crows in that their highs and lows are each consecutively lower. The last day completely erases the small black days and closes inside the gap between the first and second days.

Bearish Breakaway

The bearish Breakaway pattern involves a gap in the direction of the trend followed by three consecutively higher price days (Figure 3-85). In an uptrend, a long white day is formed. Then the next day, prices gap upward to form another white day. This is followed by two more days which set higher prices. The color of the days should be white with only one exception: the third day of the pattern, or the second day after the gap, may be either black or white as long as a new high price has been made. The low prices set in the three days after the gap should also be higher than each previous day's low price. The idea of this pattern is that prices have accelerated in the direction of trend and an overbought situation is developing. The last day sets up the trend reversal by closing inside the gap of the first and second days.

Japanese literature does not discuss a bearish version of the Breakaway pattern. I decided to test such a pattern and have found that it works quite well. See Chapter 6 for results.

Rules of Recognition

1. The first day is a long day with color representing the current trend.

2. The second day is the same color and the body gaps in the direction of the trend.

3. The third and fourth days continue the trend direction, with closes consecutively greater in the direction of trend.

4. The fifth day is a long opposite-color day that closes inside the gap caused by the first and second days.

Scenarios and Psychology Behind the Pattern

It is important to realize what is being accomplished here: the trend has accelerated with a big gap and then starts to fizzle, but it still moves in the same direction. The slow deterioration of the trend is quite evident from this pattern. Finally, a burst in the opposite direction completely recovers the previous three days' price action. What causes the reversal implication is that the gap has not been filled. A short-term reversal has taken place.

Pattern Flexibility

Because this is a complex pattern, it is difficult to discuss flexibility. As long as the basic premise is maintained, this pattern can offer some flexibility. There could be more than three days after the gap as long as the last day of the pattern closes inside the initial gap. It is also possible to have at least two days after the gap.

Pattern Breakdown

Figure 3-86   **Figure 3-87**

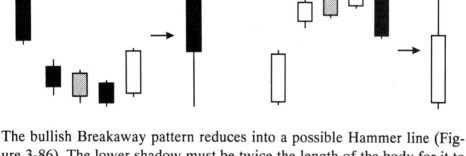

The bullish Breakaway pattern reduces into a possible Hammer line (Figure 3-86). The lower shadow must be twice the length of the body for it to qualify as a Hammer. This is quite possible if the gap on the second day is large and followed by significantly lower prices on days three and four. This, of course, supports the pattern.

The bearish Breakaway pattern reduces to a long candle line with a white body at the lower end of its range (Figure 3-87). Chances are that this would not be a Shooting Star because of the large gap on the second day and the higher prices that followed. It seems that the bearish Breakaway would require further confirmation before selling.

Related Patterns

Because of this pattern's complexity, there are no related patterns.

Examples

Figure 3-88A

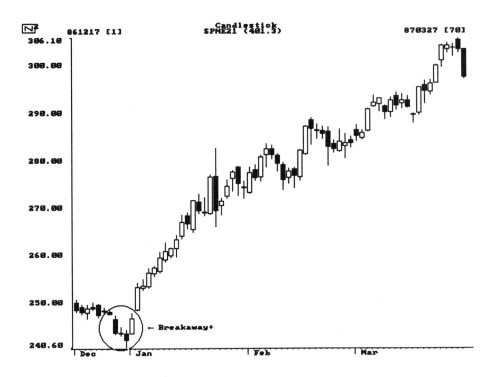

Figure 3-88B

Two Crows

(*niwa garasu*)
Bearish reversal pattern.
Confirmation is suggested.

Figure 3-89

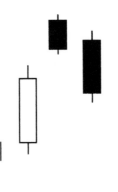

Commentary

This pattern is good only as a topping reversal or bearish pattern. The uptrend is supported by a long white day. The next day gaps much higher, but closes near its low which is still above the body of the first day. The next (third) day opens inside the body of the second black day, then sells off into the body of the first day. This has closed the gap and given us the same pattern as a Dark Cloud Cover if the last two days of the Two Crows pattern were combined into a single candle line. The fact that this gap was filled so quickly somewhat eliminates the traditional gap analysis, which would indicate a continuation of the trend.

Rules of Recognition

1. The trend continues with a long white day.

2. The second day is a gap up and a black day.

3. The third day is also a black day.

4. The third day opens inside the body of the second day and closes inside the body of the first day.

Scenarios and Psychology Behind the Pattern

The market has had an extended up move. A gap higher followed by a lower close for the second day shows that there is some weakness in the rally. The third day opens higher, but not above the open of the previous day, and then sells off. This sell-off closes well into the body of the first day. This action fills the gap after only the second day. The bullishness has to be eroding quickly.

Pattern Flexibility

The Two Crows pattern is slightly more bearish than the Upside Gap Two Crows pattern. The third day is a long black day which needs to close only inside the body of the first day. The longer this black day is and the lower it closes into the first day, the more bearish it is.

Pattern Breakdown

Figure 3-90

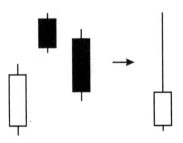

The Two Crows pattern reduces to a possible Shooting Star line (Figure 3-90). This would support the bearishness of the Two Crows pattern.

Related Patterns

The Two Crows pattern is similar to the Dark Cloud Cover in that it represents a short-term top in the market. If the second and third days were combined into one, the pattern would become a Dark Cloud Cover. The Upside Gap Two Crows is slightly different in that the third day does not close into the body of the first day. It also is a weak version of the Evening Star, except that there is no gap between the second and third bodies.

Example

Figure 3-91

Three Inside Up and Three Inside Down

(*harami age* and *harami sage*)
No confirmation is required.

Figure 3-92

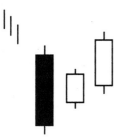

Figure 3-93

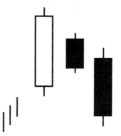

Commentary

The Three Inside Up and Three Inside Down patterns are confirmations for the Harami pattern. As shown in Figures 3-92 and 3-93, the first two days are exactly the same as the Harami. The third day is a confirming close day with respect to the bullish or bearish case. A bullish Harami followed by a third day that closes higher would be a Three Inside Up pattern. Similarly, a bearish Harami with a lower close on the third day would be a Three Inside Down pattern.

The Three Inside Up and Three Inside Down patterns are not found in any Japanese literature. I developed them to assist in improving the overall results of the Harami pattern, which they have done quite well.

Rules of Recognition

1. A Harami pattern is first identified using all previously set rules.

2. The third day shows a higher close for a Three Inside Up and a lower close for a Three Inside Down.

Scenarios and Psychology Behind the Pattern

This pattern, being a confirmation for the Harami, can represent the success of the Harami pattern only by moving in the forecast direction.

Pattern Flexibility

Because this pattern is a confirmation of the Harami pattern, the flexibility would be the same as that of the Harami. The amount of engulfment and size of the second day helps to strengthen or weaken this pattern, as the case may be.

Pattern Breakdown

Figure 3-94   **Figure 3-95**

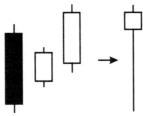   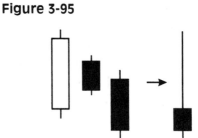

The bullish Three Inside Up pattern reduces to a bullish Hammer which supports the pattern (Figure 3-94). The bearish Three Inside Down reduces to a bearish Shooting Star line, which also supports it (Figure 3-95).

Related Patterns

The Harami pattern and Harami Cross pattern are part of these patterns.

Examples

Figure 3-96A

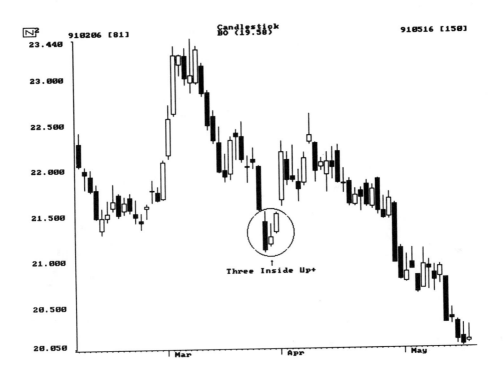

Figure 3-96B

Three Outside Up and Three Outside Down

(*tsutsumi age* and *tsutsumi sage*)
No confirmation is required.

Figure 3-97

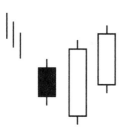

Figure 3-98

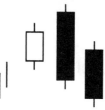

Commentary

The Three Outside Up and Three Outside Down patterns (Figures 3-97 and 3-98) are confirmations for the Engulfing patterns. The concept is identical to the Three Inside Up and Three Inside Down patterns and how they worked with the Harami. Here, the Engulfing pattern is followed by either a higher or a lower close on the third day, depending on whether the pattern is up or down.

The Three Outside Up and Three Outside Down patterns are not found in any Japanese literature. I developed them to assist in improving the overall results of the Engulfing pattern, which they have done quite well.

Pattern Recognition

1. An Engulfing pattern is formed using all of the previously set rules.

2. The third day has a higher close for the Three Outside Up pattern and a lower close for a Three Outside Down pattern.

Scenarios and Psychology Behind the Pattern

These patterns, representing the confirmation of the Engulfing pattern, can only show the success of the forecast of the appropriate Engulfing pattern.

Pattern Flexibility

Confirmation patterns do not have any more flexibility than the underlying pattern. The amount of confirmation made on the last day can influence the magnitude of this pattern's forecast.

Pattern Breakdown

Figure 3-99   **Figure 3-100**

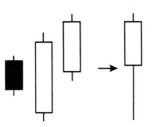
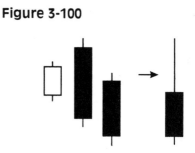

The bullish Three Outside Up pattern reduces to a possible Hammer line (Figure 3-99), and the bearish Three Outside Down reduces to a possible Shooting Star line (Figure 3-100). The word possible is used here because the difference between the first day's open and the third day's close can be significant, which would negate the Hammer and Shooting Star lines. The supporting point is that the body will be the color of the sentiment.

Related Patterns

The Engulfing pattern is a subpart of this pattern.

Examples

Figure 3-101A

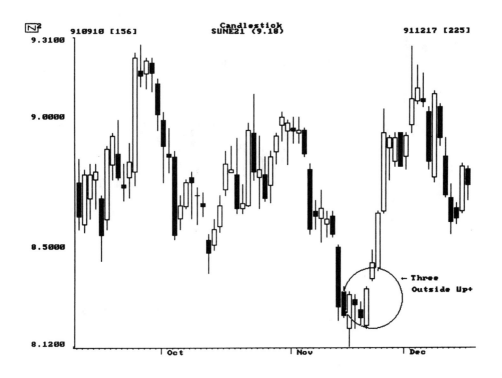

Figure 3-101B

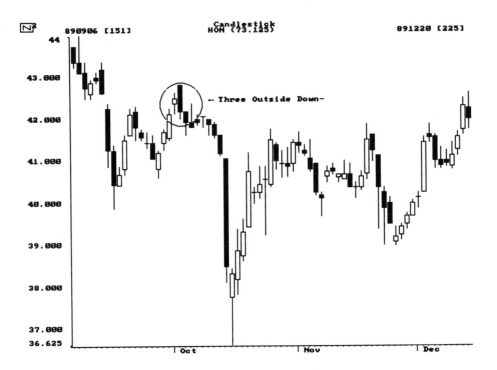

Three Stars in the South

(*kyoku no santen boshi*)
Bullish reversal pattern.
Confirmation is suggested.

Figure 3-102

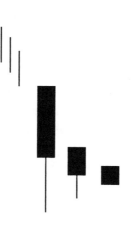

Commentary

This pattern shows a downtrend slowly deteriorating with less and less daily price movement and consecutively higher lows (Figure 3-102). The long lower shadow on the first day is critical to this pattern because it is the first sign of buying enthusiasm. The next day opens higher, trades lower, but does not go lower than the previous day's low. This second day also closes off of its low. The third day is a Black Marubozu and is engulfed by the previous day's range.

Rules of Recognition

1. The first day is a long black day with a long lower shadow (Hammer-like).

2. The second day has the same basic shape as the first day, only smaller. The low is above the previous day's low.

119

3. The third day is a small Black Marubozu that opens and closes inside the previous day's range.

Scenarios and Psychology Behind the Pattern

A downtrend has continued when, after a new low has been made, a rally closes well above the low. This will cause some concern among the shorts because it represents buying, something that has not been happening until now. The second day opens higher, which lets some longs get out of their positions. However, that is the high for the day. Trading is lower, but not lower than the previous day, which causes a rally to close above the low. The bears are certainly concerned now because of the higher low. The last day is a day of indecision, with hardly any price movement. Anyone who is still short will not want to see anything more to the up side.

Pattern Flexibility

The last day of this pattern could have small shadows that probably would not greatly affect the outcome. Basically, each consecutive day is engulfed by the previous day's range.

Pattern Breakdown

Figure 3-103

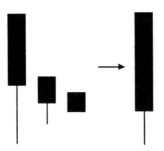

This pattern reduces to a long black line, which normally is quite bearish (Figure 3-103). Because of this conflict, definite confirmation should be required.

Related Patterns

This is somewhat like the Three Black Crows, except that the lows are not lower and the last day is not a long body. Of course, this pattern has a bullish implication, whereas the Three Black Crows pattern is bearish.

Example

Figure 3-104

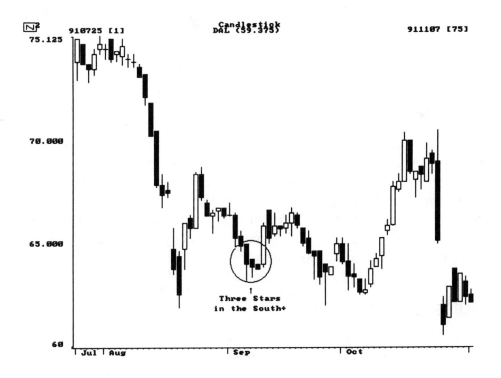

Concealing Baby Swallow

(*kotsubame tsutsumi*)
Bullish reversal pattern.
No confirmation is required.

Figure 3-105

Commentary

Two Black Marubozu days support the strength of the downtrend (Figure 3-105). On the third day, the downtrend begins to deteriorate, with a period of trading above the open price. This is especially important because the open was gapped down from the previous day's close. The fourth day completely engulfs the third day, including the upper shadow. Even though the close is at a new low, the velocity of the previous downtrend has eroded significantly and shorts should be protected.

Rules of Recognition

1. Two Black Marubozu days make up the first two days of this pattern.

2. The third day is black with a down gap open. However, this day trades into the body of the previous day, producing a long upper shadow.

3. The fourth black day completely engulfs the third day, including the shadow.

Scenarios and Psychology Behind the Pattern

Any time a downtrend can continue with two Black Marubozu days, the bears must be excited. Then on the third day, the open is gapped down, which also adds to the excitement. However, trading during this day goes above the close of the previous day and causes some real concern about the downtrend, even though the day closes at or near its low. The next day opens significantly higher with a gap. After the opening, however, the market sells off and closes at a new low. This last day has given the shorts an excellent opportunity to cover their short positions.

Pattern Flexibility

This is a very strict pattern and does not allow much in the way of flexibility. The gap between the second and third day is necessary, and the upper shadow of the third day must extend into the previous day's body. In addition the fourth day must completely engulf the previous day's range. To meet all of these requirements, only a few changes in relative size can be allowed.

Pattern Breakdown

This pattern reduces to a long black day which is almost always considered a bearish day (Figure 3-106). Because of this direct conflict, confirmation is required.

Figure 3-106

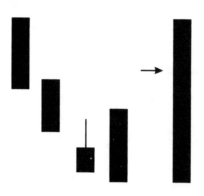

Related Patterns

Concealing Baby Swallow resembles the Three Black Crows here, as did the Three Stars in the South pattern. However, the Three Black Crows is a bearish pattern and must be in an uptrend to be valid, whereas this pattern occurs in a downtrend. This pattern starts out much like the Ladder Bottom pattern.

Example

Figure 3-107

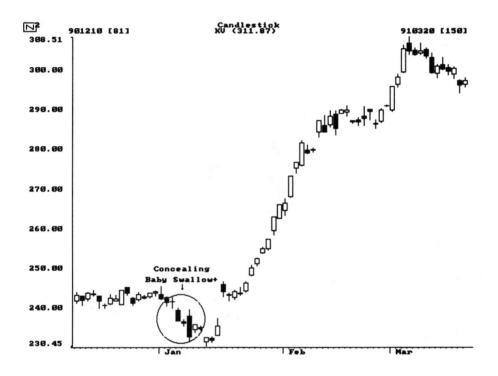

Stick Sandwich

(*gyakusashi niten zoko*)
Bullish reversal pattern.
Confirmation is suggested.

Figure 3-108

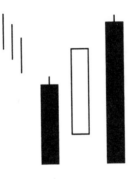

Commentary

In the Stick Sandwich pattern two black bodies have a white body between them (Figure 3-108). The closing prices of the two black bodies must be equal. A support price has been found and the opportunity for prices to reverse is quite good.

Rules of Recognition

1. A black body in a downtrend is followed by a white body that trades above the close of the black body.

2. The third day is a black day with a close equal to the first day.

Scenarios and Psychology Behind the Pattern

A good downtrend is under way. Prices open higher on the next trading day and then trade higher all day, closing at or near the high. This action suggests that the previous downtrend has probably reversed and that shorts should be protected, if not covered. The next day, prices open even higher, which should cause some covering initially, but then prices drift lower to close at the same price as two days ago. Anyone who does not note support and resistance points in the market is taking exceptional risk. Another day of trading should tell the story.

Pattern Flexibility

Some Japanese references use the low prices as the support point for the two black days. Using the close price presents a more memorable support point and therefore a better chance of reversal.

Pattern Breakdown

Figure 3-109

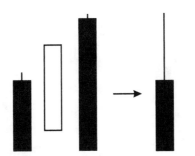

The Stick Sandwich breaks down to an Inverted Hammer line as long as the body of the first day is considerable smaller than the range of the third day (Figure 3-109). If the first day is a small body and the third day's price range (high to low) is two or three times that of the first day, this pattern reduces to the bullish Inverted Hammer. However, if this does not occur, the Stick Sandwich reduces to a black line, which is usually bearish. As a result, confirmation is suggested.

Related Patterns

The last two days of this pattern are similar to a bearish Engulfing pattern in most instances. It would have to be seen if the support point is better than the bearish candle pattern, assuming no consideration is made to the previous trend.

Examples

Figure 3-110

Kicking

(keri ashi)
No confirmation is required.

Figure 3-111

Figure 3-112

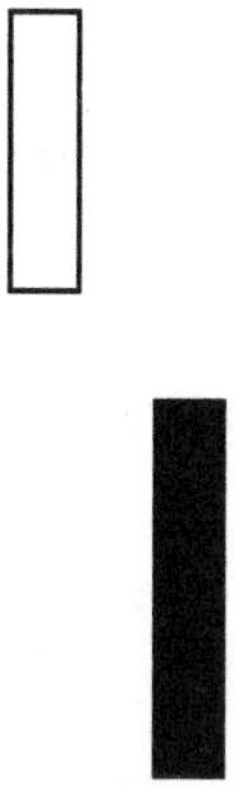

Commentary

The Kicking pattern is similar to the Separating Lines pattern, except that instead of the open prices being equal, a gap occurs. The bullish Kicking pattern is a Black Marubozu followed by a White Marubozu (Figure 3-111). The bearish Kicking pattern is a White Marubozu followed by a Black Marubozu (Figure 3-112). Some Japanese theory says that future movement will be in the direction of the longer side of the two candles, regardless of the price trend. The market direction is not as important with this pattern as it is with most other candle patterns.

Rules of Recognition

1. A Marubozu of one color is followed by a Marubozu of the opposite color.

2. A gap must occur between the two lines.

Scenarios and Psychology Behind the Pattern

The market has been in a trend when prices gap the next day. The prices never enter into the previous day's range and then close with another gap.

Pattern Flexibility

This allows no flexibility. If the gap does not exist, a Separating Lines (continuation) pattern will be formed.

Pattern Breakdown

Figure 3-113   **Figure 3-114**

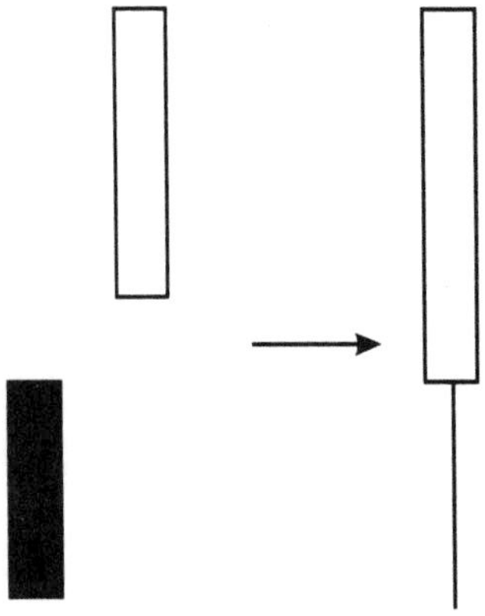

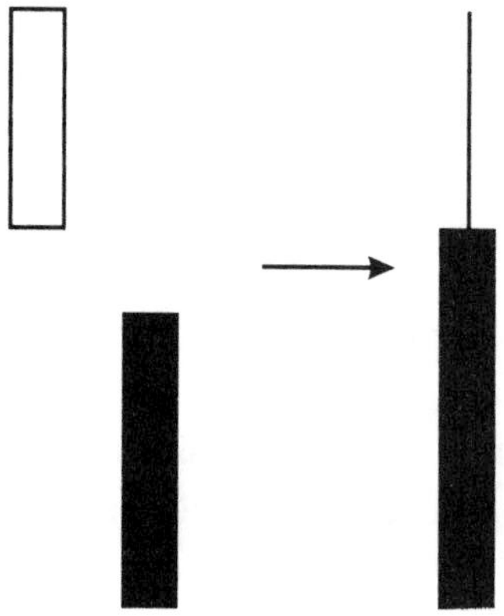

The bullish Kicking pattern reduces to a long white candle line, which usually is bullish (Figure 3-113). The bearish Kicking pattern reduces to a long black candle line, which is usually bearish (Figure 3-114).

Related Patterns

The Separating Lines pattern is almost the same, except for the gap and the fact that the Separating Lines is a continuation pattern.

Example

Figure 3-115

Homing Pigeon

(*shita banare kobato gaeshi*)
Bullish reversal pattern.
Confirmation is suggested.

Commentary

The Homing Pigeon closely resembles the Harami pattern, except that both
its bodies are black rather than opposite in color.

Figure 3-116

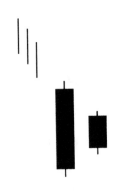

Rules of Recognition

1. A long black body occurs in a downtrend.

2. A short black body is completely inside the previous day's body.

Scenarios and Psychology Behind the Pattern

The market is in a downtrend, evidenced by a long black day. The next day, prices open higher, trade completely within the prior day's body, and then close slightly lower. Depending upon the severity of the previous trend, this shows a deterioration and offers an opportunity to get out of the market.

Pattern Flexibility

Two-day patterns do not offer much flexibility.

Pattern Breakdown

The Homing Pigeon pattern reduces to a long black candle line with a lower shadow, which certainly is not a bullish line (Figure 3-117). Confirmation would definitely be suggested.

Figure 3-117

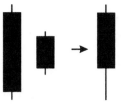

Related Patterns

The Harami is similar in its candle line relationship, but both of its days must be black.

Example

Figure 3-118

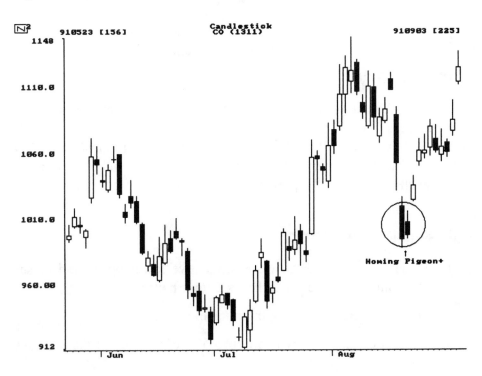

Ladder Bottom

(*hashigo gaeshi*)
Bullish reversal pattern.
Confirmation is suggested.

Figure 3-119

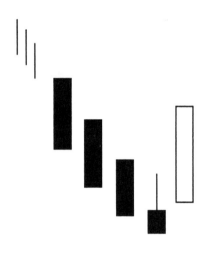

Commentary

After a reasonable downtrend with four consecutive lower closes and black days, the market trades higher than the open (Figure 3-119). This action is the first indication of buying even though the market still closes at a new low. On the next day, prices gap higher and never look back. The last day closes much higher than the previous day or two.

Rules of Recognition

1. Three long black days with consecutive lower opens and closes occur much like the Three Black Crows pattern.

2. The fourth day is black with an upper shadow.

3. The last day is white with an open above the body of the previous day.

Scenarios and Psychology Behind the Pattern

A downtrend has been in place for some time and the bears are sure to be complacent. After a good move to the downside, prices trade above the open price and almost reach the high price of the previous day, but then they close at another new low. This action certainly will get the attention of the shorts and shows that the market will not go down forever. The shorts will rethink their positions and, if profits are good, the next day they will sell. This action causes a gap up on the last day of the pattern and the close is considerably higher. If volume is high on the last day, a trend reversal has probably occurred.

Pattern Flexibility

The four black days of the Ladder Bottom pattern may or may not be long but consecutively lower closes must occur. The last day must be white and may be either long or short, as long as the close is above the previous day's high.

Pattern Breakdown

Figure 3-120

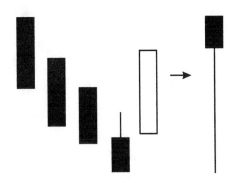

The Ladder Bottom reduces to a Hammer pattern, which supports its bullish implications (Figure 3-120).

Related Patterns

The Ladder Bottom starts out just like the Concealing Baby Swallow pattern. The first three days also resemble the Three Black Crows pattern except that a downtrend is in place.

Example

Figure 3-121

Matching Low

(niten zoko/kenuki)
Bullish reversal pattern.
Confirmation is suggested.

Figure 3-122

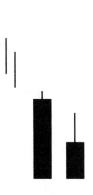

Commentary

The Matching Low pattern follows a concept similar to that used in the Stick Sandwich pattern. In fact, by removing the middle day in the Stick Sandwich pattern, you will get a Matching Low pattern. A long black day continues the downtrend, the next day opens higher, but then closes at the same close of the previous day. This yields two black days together with their lower bodies (closes) equal. This pattern indicates a bottom has been made, even though the new low was tested and there was no follow through, which is indicative of a good support price.

Rules of Recognition

1. A long black day occurs.

2. The second day is also a black day with its close equal to the close of the first day.

Scenarios and Psychology Behind the Pattern

The market has been trading lower, as evidenced by another long black day. The next day, prices open higher, trade still higher, and then close at the same price as before. This is a classic indication of short-term support and will cause much concern from any apathetic bears who ignore it. Apathetic bears are short the market, and quite comfortable with their short position. If they ignore the Matching Low as a possible trend reversal, it will cause them much concern.

An interesting concept is presented with this pattern. The psychology of the market is not necessarily with the action behind the daily trading, but with the fact that the trading closes at the same price on both days.

Pattern Flexibility

The length of the bodies of the two days may be either long or short without affecting on the meaning of the pattern.

Pattern Breakdown

Figure 3-123

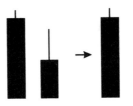

The Matching Low pattern reduces to a long black line, which is usually bearish (Figure 3-123). Confirmation would be highly recommended.

Related Patterns

The Matching Low closely resembles the Homing Pigeon pattern, but, because the closes are equal, the second day does not quite fit the definition of being engulfed.

Examples

Figure 3-124

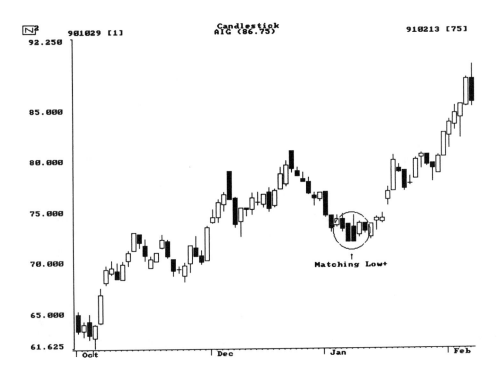

4 | Continuation Patterns

Continuation patterns are included in a separate chapter from reversal patterns only to make later reference easier. Keep in mind that once a pattern has been identified, it is suggesting a direction for future price movement. It really doesn't matter if that future price movement is the same as before or a reversal. Continuation patterns, according to the Sakata Method, are a time of rest in the market. Whatever the pattern, you must make a decision on your current position, even if that decision is to stay where you are.

The format of discussion for this chapter is identical to that of the previous chapter on reversal candle patterns. In condensed form, that format is

- **Pattern name**
- **Japanese name and interpretation**
- **Commentary**
- **Graphic of classic pattern(s)**
- **Rules of recognition**
- **Scenarios / psychology behind the pattern**
- **Pattern flexibility**

- **Pattern breakdown**

- **Related patterns**

- **Examples**

Continuation Pattern Index

Upside Tasuki Gap
and Downside Tasuki Gap

(*uwa banare tasuki* and *shita banare tasuki*)
Confirmation is recommended.

Figure 4-1   **Figure 4-2**

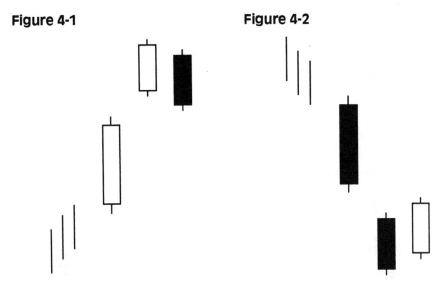

Commentary

The typical Tasuki line occurs when the price opens lower from a white line and then closes lower than the previous day's low. When the price opens higher from a black day's close and then closes higher than its high is the opposite case. Tasuki lines are mentioned in a number of sources of candlestick literature, but they do not contribute enough to be considered as individual patterns. A Tasuki is a sash for holding up sleeves. The Tasuki Gaps involve the Tasuki line after a gap in the direction of the current market trend.

An Upside Tasuki Gap (Figure 4-1) is a white candlestick which has gapped above the previous white candlestick, then followed by a black candlestick that closes inside that gap. This last day must also open inside the second white day's body. An important point is that the gap made between the first two days is not filled. The philosophy is that one should go long on the close of the last day. The same concept would be true in reverse for a Downside Tasuki Gap (Figure 4-2).

Rules of Recognition

1. A trend is under way, with a gap between two candlesticks of the same color.

2. The color of the first two candlesticks represents the prevailing trend.

3. The third day, an opposite-color candlestick opens within the body of the second day.

4. The third day closes into the gap but does not fully close the gap.

Scenarios and Psychology Behind the Pattern

The psychology behind a Tasuki Gap is quite simple: Go with the trend of the gap. The correction day (the third day) did not fill the gap and the previous trend should continue. This is looked upon as temporary profit taking. The Japanese widely follow gaps (windows). Therefore, the fact that the gap does not get filled or closed means that the previous trend should resume.

The literature is sometimes contradictory on gaps. One normally expects a gap to provide support and/or resistance. The fact that the gap is tested so quickly is reason to believe that the gap may not provide its usual analytic ability.

Pattern Flexibility

The first day's color is not as important as the color of the second and third days. It is best that it be the same color as the second day, which would fully support the ongoing trend.

Pattern Breakdown

Figure 4-3   **Figure 4-4**

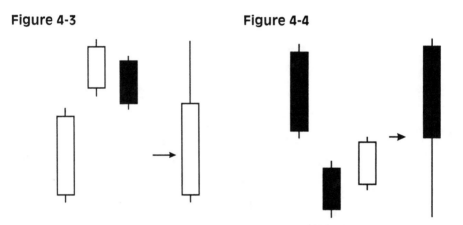

The Upside Tasuki Gap pattern reduces into a long line with a white body at the lower end (Figure 4-3). The only support here can be in the fact that the breakdown is a long white line which is normally considered bullish. The Downside Tasuki Gap reduces to a long black line which is usually bearish. Because of the lack of strong support, further confirmation is recommended.

Related Patterns

The Tasuki lines by themselves are somewhat opposite of the Piercing Line and the Dark Cloud Cover, which are reversal patterns. The Upside and Downside Tasuki Gap patterns are very similar to the Upside and Downside Gap Three Methods patterns discussed later in this chapter. You will see that they are also in direct conflict with each other. It might be best to see the statistical results of the pattern testing in later chapters.

Examples

Figure 4-5A

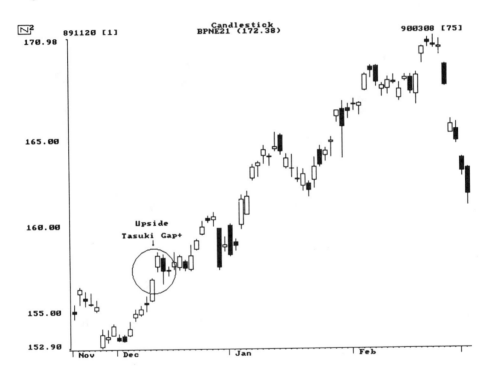

Figure 4-5B

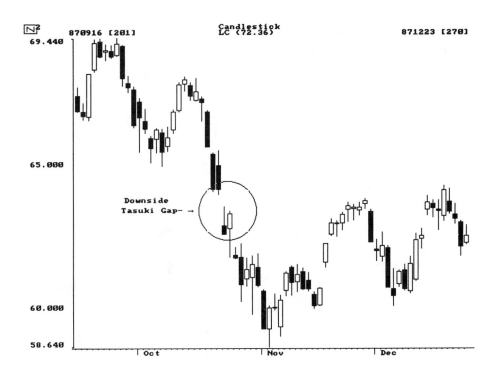

Side-by-Side White Lines

(narabi aka)
No confirmation is required for the bullish case, but confirmation is recommended for the bearish lines.

Figure 4-6   **Figure 4-7**

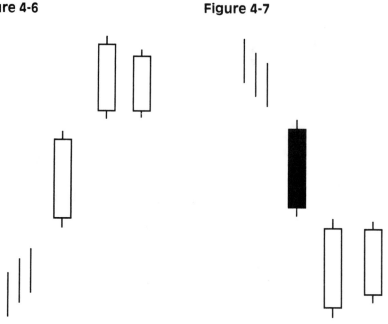

Commentary

Narabi means "in a row" and *narabiaka* means "whites in a row." The Japanese literature refers to Side-by-Side Lines, both black and white, but only indicates a pause or a stalemate when they are by themselves. The pattern of importance here is two white lines that have gapped in the direction of the current trend.

Bullish Side-by-Side White Lines

Two white candlesticks of similar size are side-by-side after gapping above another white candlestick. Not only are they of similar size, but the opening price should be very close. The Bullish Side-by Side White Lines (Figure 4-6) is also referred to as an Upside Gap Side-by-Side White Lines (*uwappanare narabiaka*).

Bearish Side-by-Side White Lines

Side-by-Side White Lines which gap to the downside are very rare. These are also called Downside Gap Side-by-Side White Lines (Figure 4-7). Despite what appears to be obvious, these two white lines are looked upon as short covering. This action, like many continuation patterns, represents the market taking a rest or buying time.

It would be a normal expectation to have two Side-by-Side Black Lines for this continuation pattern. A downside gap to Side-by-Side Black Lines would certainly indicate a continuation of the downtrend. This pattern, however, is not of much use because it portrays the obvious. Another derivation of these lines would be Side-by-Side White Lines which do not gap, but are in an uptrending market. These are called Side-by-Side White Lines in Stalemate (*ikizumari narabiaka*). These indicate that the market is approaching its top and with limited support.

Rules of Recognition

1. A gap is made in the direction of the trend.

2. The second day is a white candle line.

3. The third day is also a white candle line of about the same size and opens at about the same price.

Scenarios and Psychology Behind the Pattern

Bullish Side-by-Side White Lines

The market is in a uptrend. A long white candlestick is formed, which further perpetuates the bullishness. The next day, the market gaps up on the open and closes still higher. However, on the third day, the market opens much lower, in fact, as low as the previous day's open. The initial selling that caused the lower open ends quickly and the market climbs to yet another high. This demonstrates the force behind the buyers, and the rally should continue.

Bearish Side-by-Side White Lines

A downtrend is further enhanced with a long black candle line followed by a large downward gap open on the next day. The market trades higher all day, but not high enough to close the gap. The third day opens lower, at about the same open as the second day. Because of the resistance to further downside action, shorts are covered, causing the third day also to rally and close higher, but again not high enough to close the gap. If enough short covering was accomplished and the rally attempt was not very convincing, the downtrend should continue.

Pattern Flexibility

Because Side-by-Side White Lines are used only after gapping, there is not much flexibility in this pattern. The two white lines should be of similar body length, but this length is not as important as the fact that they gapped in the direction of the trend. Their open prices should be close to the same, though.

Pattern Breakdown

Figure 4-8   **Figure 4-9**

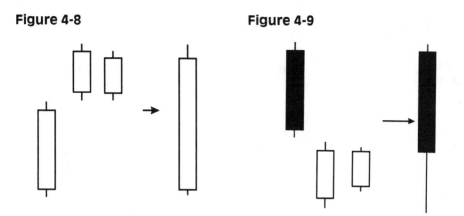

The Upside Gap Side-by-Side White Lines reduce to a long white candlestick which fully supports the bullish continuation (Figure 4-8). The Downside Gap Side-by-Side White Lines reduce to a black candlestick with a long lower shadow (Figure 4-9). This single candle line does not fully support the bearish continuation and suggests further confirmation.

Related Patterns

There are no patterns comparable to the Side-by-Side White Lines. The Breakaway pattern has some similarities in that the second and third days gap in the direction of trend.

Examples

Figure 4-10A

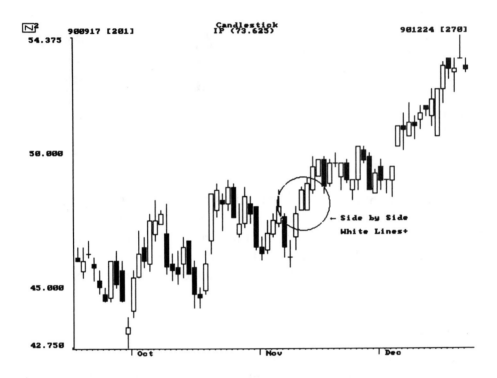

Figure 4-10B

Rising Three Methods and Falling Three Methods

(*uwa banare sanpoo ohdatekomi* and *shita banare sanpoo ohdatekomi*)
No confirmation is required.

Figure 4-11   **Figure 4-12**

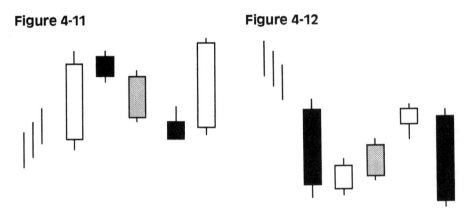

Commentary

The Three Methods (Chapter 5) include the bullish Rising Three Methods and the bearish Falling Three Methods. Both are continuation patterns that represent breaks in the trend of prices without causing a reversal. They are days of rest in the market action and can be used to add to positions, if already in the market.

Rising Three Methods

A long white candlestick is formed in an uptrend (Figure 4-11). After this long day, a group of small-bodied candlesticks occur which show some resistance to the previous trend. These reaction days are generally black, but most importantly, their bodies all fall within the high-low range of the first long white day. Remember that the high-low range includes the shadows. The final candlestick (normally the fifth day) opens above the close of the previous reaction day and then closes at a new high.

Falling Three Methods

The Falling Three Methods pattern is the bearish counterpart of the Rising Three Methods pattern. A downtrend is underway, when it is further perpetuated with a long black candlestick (Figure 4-12). The next three days produce small-body days that move against the trend. It is best if the bodies of these reactionary days are white. It is noted that the bodies all remain within the high-low range of the first black candlestick. The next and last days should open near the previous day's close and then close at a new low. The market's rest is over.

Rules of Recognition

1. A long candlestick is formed representing the current trend.

2. This candlestick is followed by a group of small real body candlesticks. It is best if they are opposite in color.

3. The small candlesticks rise or fall opposite to the trend and remain within the high-low range of the first day.

4. The final day should be a strong day, with a close outside of the first day's close and in the direction of the original trend.

Scenarios and Psychology Behind the Pattern

The concept behind the Rising Three Methods comes from early Japanese futures trading history and is a vital part of the Sakata Method. The Three Methods pattern is considered a rest from trading or a rest from battle. In modern terminology, the market is just taking a break. The psychology behind a move like this is that some doubt creeps in about the ability of the trend to continue. This doubt increases as the small-range reaction days take place. However, once the bulls see that a new low cannot be made, the bullishness is resumed and new highs are set quickly. The Falling Three Methods pattern is just the opposite.

Pattern Flexibility

Because this pattern normally consists of five candle lines, it is somewhat rare to find in its classic form. Some leeway can be allowed in the range of the reaction days. They may go slightly above or below the range of the first day. It is best, if this is allowed, that they cover the range of the first day completely. If they do not and tend in one direction, the pattern can become a Mat Hold pattern, if it occurs in an uptrend.

Pattern Breakdown

Figure 4-13   **Figure 4-14**

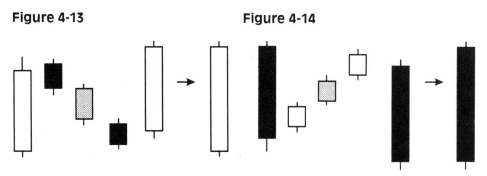

The Rising Three Methods pattern reduces to a long white candlestick, which fully supports the bullish continuation (Figure 4-13). The Falling Three Methods pattern reduces to a long black candlestick, which fully supports the bearish continuation (Figure 4-14).

Related Patterns

A pattern similar to the bullish Rising Three Methods is the Mat Hold pattern. It is also a bullish continuation pattern but allows greater flexibility in the reaction days. That is, the small black days that are between the two long white days do not have to be within the range of the first white day. These reaction days are generally higher relative to the first candlestick. Seeing the two patterns side-by-side will show that the uptrend was, and is, much stronger for the Mat Hold pattern.

Examples

Figure 4-15A

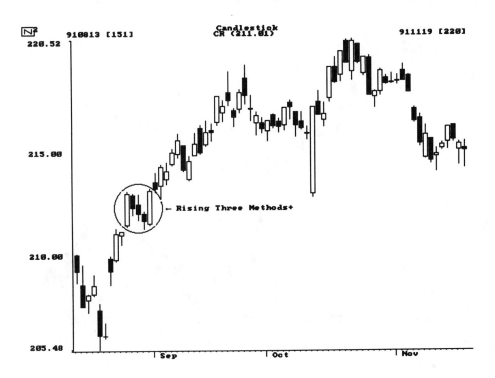

Figure 4-15B

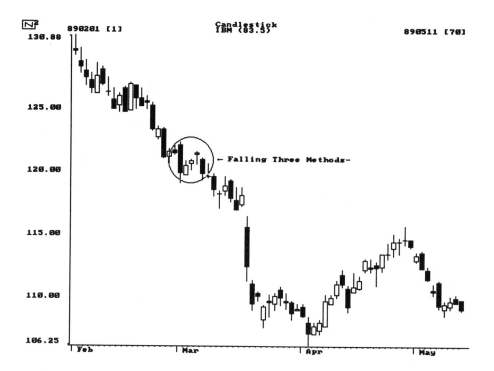

Separating Lines

(iki chigai sen)
Confirmation is required, especially for the bullish case.

Figure 4-16   **Figure 4-17**

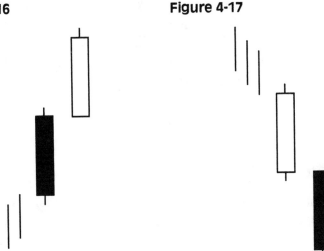

Commentary

The Separating Lines have the same open and are opposite in color. They are similar, but opposite of the Meeting Lines. The second day of these patterns is a Belt Hold candlestick. The bullish pattern (Figure 4-16) has a white bullish Belt Hold and the bearish pattern (Figure 4-17) has a black bearish Belt Hold. *Ikichigaisen* means lines that move in opposite directions. Sometimes these are called Dividing *(furiwake)* Lines.

Rules of Recognition

1. The first day is the opposite color of the current trend.

2. The second day is the opposite color of the first.

3. The two bodies meet in the middle, at the open price.

Scenarios and Psychology Behind the Pattern

An uptrend is in place when a long black day occurs. This is not normal for a strong market and will produce some skepticism. However, the next day opens much higher, in fact, it opens at the previous black day's opening price. Prices then move higher for the rest of the day and close higher, which suggests that the prior uptrend should now continue. This scenario is for the bullish Separating Line; the bearish scenario is quite similar, but opposite.

Pattern Flexibility

Separating Lines should each be long lines: however, there is no requirement that this be so. Strong *furiwake* lines would be two long bodies without any shadows (*marubozu*) at the points where they meet.

Pattern Breakdown

Figure 4-18   **Figure 4-19**

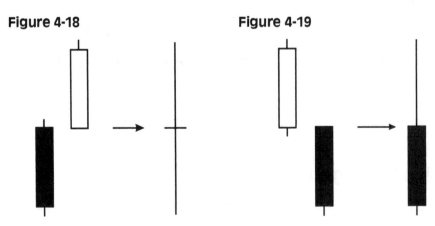

The bullish Separating Lines pattern reduces to a Long-Legged Doji line (Figure 4-18). A Doji, and especially the Long-Legged Doji, represents indecision in the market and therefore does not fully support the bullish continuation of this pattern. The bearish Separating Lines pattern reduces to a candle line with a black body near the lower portion of the range (Figure 4-19). This line can be considered bearish and therefore supports the bearish continuation pattern.

Related Patterns

The Meeting Lines, which are not continuation, but reversal patterns, are similar in concept.

Examples

Figure 4-20A

Figure 4-20B

Mat Hold

(*uwa banare sante oshi*)
Bullish continuation pattern.
No confirmation is required.

Figure 4-21

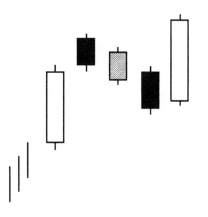

Commentary

The Mat Hold pattern is a modified version of the Rising Three Methods. The first three days start out like the Upside Gap Two Crows, with the exception that the second black body (third day) dips into the body of the first long white day (Figure 4-21). This is followed by another small black body that closes even lower, but still within the range of the first white body. The fifth day sees a large gap opening, with a strong rise to a close above the high of the highest of the three black days. This suggests that the trend will continue upward and that new positions can be taken here.

The Mat Hold Pattern shows greater strength as a continuation signal than the Rising Three Methods. The reaction days are basically higher than the ones in the Rising Three Methods. In other words, the Mat Hold does not take quite the rest, or break from trend, that the Rising Three Methods does.

Rules of Recognition

1. A long white day is formed in an uptrending market.

2. A gap up with a lower close on the second day forms almost a star-like day.

3. The following two days are reaction days similar to the Rising Three Methods.

4. The fifth day is a white day with a new closing high.

Scenarios and Psychology Behind the Pattern

The market is continuing its rise, with a long white day confirming the bullish action. The next day prices gap open and trade in a small range, only to close slightly lower. This lower close (lower than the open) is still a new closing high for the move. The bulls have only rested, even though the price action surely brings out the bears. The next couple of days cause some concern that the upward move may be in jeopardy. These days open about where the market closed on the previous day and then close slightly lower. Even by the third such day, the market is still higher than the open of the first day (a long white day). An attitude that a reversal has failed develops and prices rise again to close at a new closing high. This fully supports the bulls' case that this was just a pause in a strong upward trend.

Pattern Flexibility

The arrangement of the three small black days should show consecutive declines, much like the Rising Three Methods. The reaction days are altogether higher than those in the Rising Three Methods.

Pattern Breakdown

The bullish Mat Hold pattern reduces to a long white candlestick, which fully supports its bullish continuation (Figure 4-22).

Figure 4-22

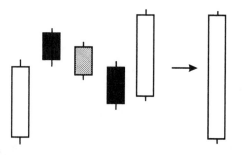

Related Patterns

Rising Three Methods is a more rigid pattern. Even though this pattern begins somewhat like the Upside Gap Two Crows, the closing of the third day into the body of the first day eliminates that possibility. One must also be on guard for a possible Three Black Crows pattern starting with the second day, especially if it is a long day.

Examples

Figure 4-23

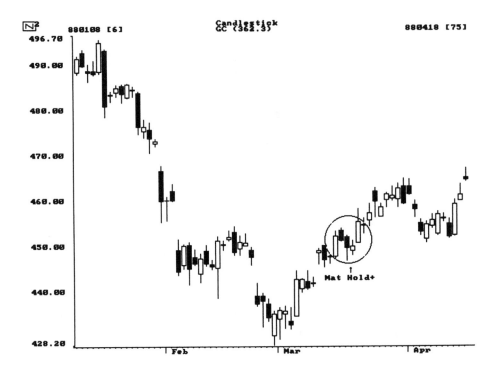

Three-Line Strike

(*sante uchi karasu no bake sen*)
Confirmation is definitely required.

Figure 4-24   **Figure 4-25**

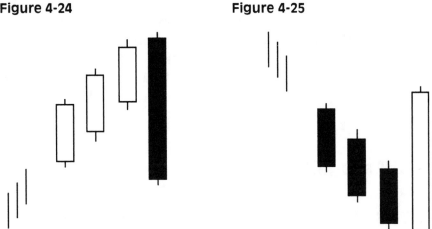

Commentary

This is a four-line pattern that appears in a defined trend. It can be looked upon as an extended version of either the Three Black Crows pattern (bearish) or the Three White Soldiers pattern (bullish). This pattern is a resting or pausing pattern; the rest is accomplished in only one day. Breaks in trend are almost always healthy for the trend. Some Japanese literature refers to this pattern as the Fooling Three Crows for the bearish version. The bullish case could also be called Fooling Three Soldiers.

Bullish Three-Line Strike

Three white days with consecutively higher highs are followed by a long black day (Figure 4-24). This long black day opens at a new high and then plummets to a lower low than the first white day of the pattern. This type of action completely erases the previous three-day upward march. If the previous trend was strong, this should be looked upon as just a setback with some profit taking. This last day is considered a liquidating day, which will give the upward trend needed strength.

Bearish Three-Line Strike

A downtrend is accentuated by three black days that each have consecutively lower lows (Figure 4-25). The fourth day opens at a new low, then rallies to close above the high of the first black day. This last long white day completely negated the previous three black days. This day should be looked upon as a day when shorts were being covered and the down move should continue.

Rules of Recognition

Bullish Three-Line Strike

1. Three days resembling Three White Soldiers are continuing an uptrend.

2. A higher open on the fourth day drops to close below the open of the first white day.

Bearish Three-Line Strike

1. Three days resembling Three Black Crows are continuing a downtrend.

2. A lower open on the fourth day rallies to close above the open of the first black day.

Scenarios and Psychology Behind the Pattern

The market has continued in its trend, aided by the recent Three Black Crows or Three White Soldiers pattern, as the case may be. The fourth day opens in the direction of the trend, but profit taking or short covering causes the market to move strongly in the opposite direction. This action causes considerable soul searching, but remember that this move completely eradicated the previous three days. This surely dried up the short-term reversal sentiment and the trend should continue in its previous direction.

Pattern Flexibility

The amount of the initial gap in the direction of trend and the amount the fourth day moved would be strong indication's of the success of this pattern as a continuation pattern.

Pattern Breakdown

Figure 4-26   **Figure 4-27**

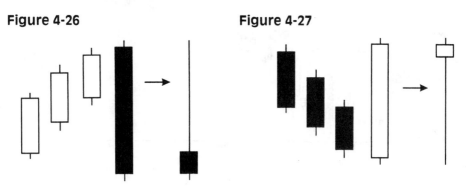

The bullish Three-Line Strike pattern reduces to a Shooting Star line and is in direct conflict with the bullishness of this pattern (Figure 4-26). The bearish Three-Line Strike pattern reduces to a Hammer and is also in direct conflict with this pattern's bearishness (Figure 4-27).

Related Patterns

There is a hint of Three White Soldiers and Three Black Crows in these patterns, but their influence is quickly negated with the strong reaction day that follows.

Chapter 4

Examples

Figure 4-28A

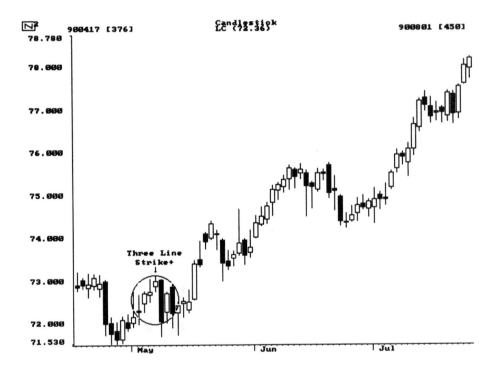

Figure 4-28B

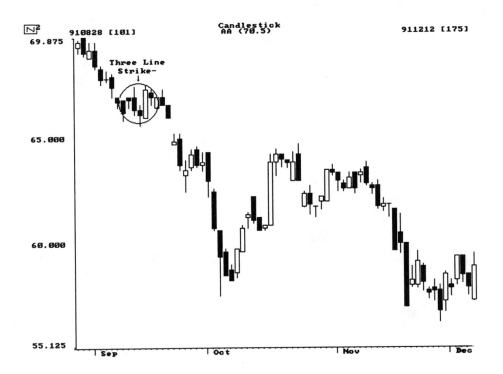

Upside Gap Three Methods and Downside Gap Three Methods

(*uwa banare sanpoo hatsu oshi* and *shita banare sanpoo ippon dachi*) Confirmation is suggested.

Figure 4-29

Figure 4-30

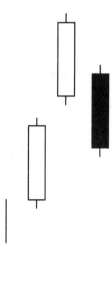

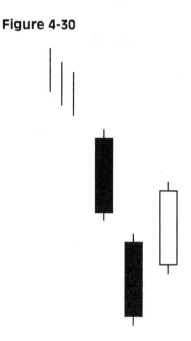

Commentary

This is a simplistic pattern, quite similar to the Upside and Downside Tasuki Gaps, that occurs in a strong trending market. A gap appears between two candlesticks of the same color (Figures 4-29 and 4-30). This color should reflect the trend of the market. The third day opens within the body of the second candlestick and then closes within the body of first candlestick (bridging the first and second candles), which would also make it the opposite color of the first two days. This would, in traditional terminology, close the gap.

Rules of Recognition

1. A trend continues, with two long days that have a gap between them.

2. The third day fills the gap and is the opposite color of the first two days.

Scenarios and Psychology Behind the Pattern

The market is moving strongly in one direction. This move is extended further by another day that gaps even more in the direction of the trend. The third day opens well into the body of the second day, then completely fills the gap. This gap-closing move should be looked upon as supporting for the current trend. Gaps normally provide excellent support and/or resistance points when considered after a reasonable period of time. Because this gap is filled within one day, some other considerations should be made. If this is the first gap of a move, then the reaction (third day) can be considered as profit taking.

Pattern Flexibility

No significant flexibility is suggested, as this is a fairly simple concept and pattern. The first day could be opposite in color to the second day without much change in the pattern's interpretation.

Pattern Breakdown

The bullish Upside Gap Three Methods pattern reduces to a Shooting Star line (Figure 4-31) and the bearish Downside Gap Three Methods pattern reduces to a Hammer line (Figure 4-32). These are two patterns (when all are considered) that do not reduce to the single line that supports the bullish or bearish nature of the pattern.

Figure 4-31   **Figure 4-32**

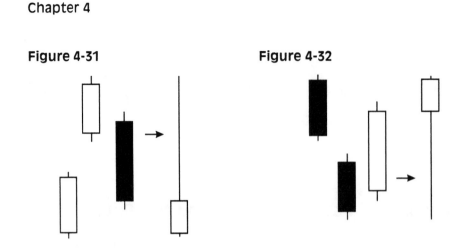

Related Patterns

These are somewhat similar to the Tasuki Gap, except that the gap is filled in the Upside and Downside Gap Three Methods. Because of this conflict in two sets of continuation patterns, one should refer to the pattern statistics found in a Chapter 7.

Examples

Figure 4-33A

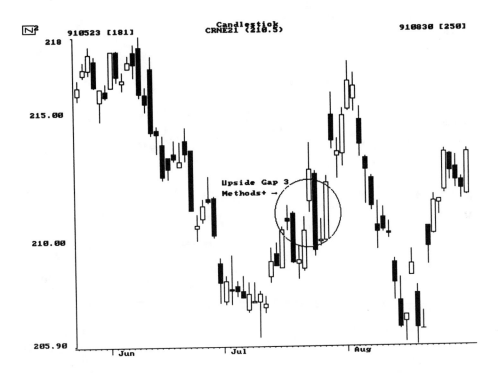

Figure 4-33B

On Neck

(*ate kubi*)
Bearish continuation pattern.
Confirmation is suggested.

Figure 4-34

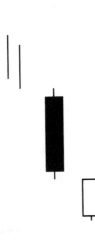

Commentary

The On Neck Line is an undeveloped version of the Piercing Line discussed in Chapter 3. A similar pattern is formed, except that the second day's white body only gets up to the previous day's low (Figure 4-34). Do not confuse this pattern with the Meeting Lines, covered in Chapter 3.

Rules of Recognition

1. A long black line is formed in a downtrend.

2. The second day is white and opens below the low of the previous day. This day does not need to be a long day or it might resemble the bullish Meeting Line.

3. The second day closes at the low of the first day.

Scenarios and Psychology Behind the Pattern

The On Neck Line usually appears during a decline. Bearishness is increased with the long black first day. The market gaps down on the second day, but cannot continue the downtrend. As the market rallies, it is stopped at the previous day's low price. This must be uncomfortable for the bottom fishers who go into the market that day. The downtrend should continue shortly.

Pattern Flexibility

If the trading volume on the second day is high, the chance of the downward trend's continuing is good.

Pattern Breakdown

Figure 4-35

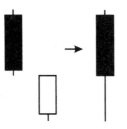

The On Neck Line pattern reduces to a fairly bearish black candlestick with a long lower shadow (Figure 4-35). This single candle line supports the bearishness of this continuation pattern.

Related Pattern

The On Neck Line pattern is a weak beginning to a Piercing Line. See also the In Neck Line and the Thrusting Line.

Examples

Figure 4-36

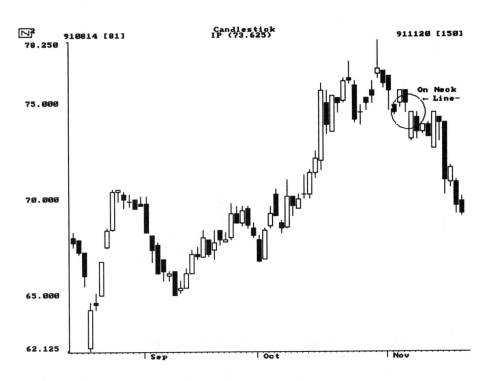

In Neck

(iri kubi)
Bearish continuation pattern.
Confirmation is suggested.

Figure 4-37

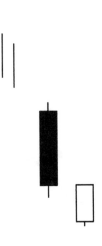

Commentary

This is also a modified or undeveloped version of the Piercing Line. The second day's white body closes near the close of the previous black day; at the lower part of the body (Figure 4-37). The actual definition requires that it close just inside the previous day's body, that is, slightly above the close. It is a higher close than the On Neck Line, but not much. If the first day's close is also at its low (Closing Marubozu), the In Neck and On Neck Lines are most probably the same.

Rules of Recognition

1. A black line develops in a downtrend.

2. The second day is a white day with an opening below the first day's low.

3. The close of the second day is just barely into the body of the first day. For all practical purposes, the closes are equal.

Scenarios and Psychology Behind the Pattern

The scenario is almost identical to the On Neck Line, except that the downtrend may not continue quite as abruptly because of the somewhat higher close.

Pattern Flexibility

If the volume on the white day (second day) is heavy, the chance of the trend's continuing is good.

Pattern Breakdown

Figure 4-38

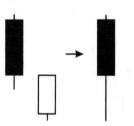

The In Neck Line pattern reduces to a black candlestick with a long lower shadow (Figure 4-38). The fact that this single line is not at all bullish lends support for the bearish continuation of this pattern.

Related Patterns

The In Neck Line, like the On Neck Line, is a weak beginning to a Piercing Line. It, however, is a little stronger, but not nearly enough to cause a reversal of trend. You should also note that this pattern, if both days are near Marubozu, would be like the Meeting Lines pattern.

Examples

Figure 4-39

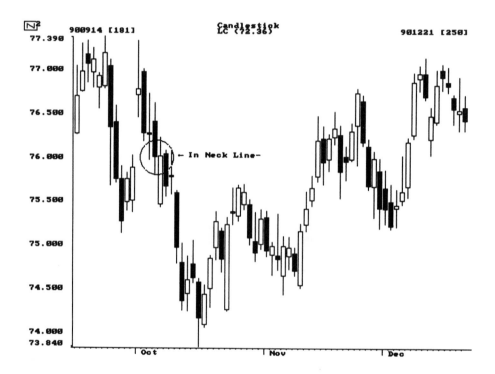

Thrusting

(*sashikomi*)
Bearish continuation pattern.
Confirmation is required.

Figure 4-40

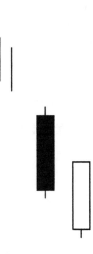

Commentary

This is the third derivative of the Piercing Line. The Thrusting Line is stronger than either the On Neck Line or the In Neck Line, but fails to close above the midpoint of the previous day's body (Figure 4-40). The second day is normally a much larger gap down than the In Neck or On Neck patterns. This makes it a long white day and confirmation definitely is needed before adding to short positions.

Rules of Recognition

1. A black day is formed in a downtrend.

2. The second day is white and opens considerably lower than the low of the first day.

3. The second day closes well into the body of the first day, but not above the midpoint.

Scenarios and Psychology Behind the Pattern

Much like the On Neck and In Neck Lines, the Thrusting Line represents a failure to rally in a down market. Because of this failure, the bulls will be discouraged and a lack of buying will let the downtrend continue.

Pattern Flexibility

Because the Thrusting pattern is approaching the bullish Piercing Line pattern and is slightly better than the On Neck Line, there is little room for flexibility.

Pattern Breakdown

Figure 4-41

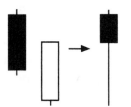

The Thrusting pattern reduces to a Hammer line which is somewhat in conflict with the bearishness of this pattern (Figure 4-41). Because the Thrusting pattern is so close to being a Piercing Line pattern, it is easy to see the possibility of no breakdown support.

Related Patterns

The Thrusting pattern is the strongest of the three lines that fail to make a Piercing Line. It is stronger than the On Neck and In Neck Lines, but weaker than the Piercing Line.

Example

Figure 4-42

Additional Note

You may wonder why there are three continuation patterns that are derived from a failure to complete a Piercing Line. The On Neck Line, In Neck Line, and Thrusting patterns all represent failed attempts to reverse the downward trend.

Why, then, are there not similar patterns that represent failed Dark Cloud Cover patterns? This can be answered by most students of the market who are familiar with normal topping and bottoming tendencies. Bottoms (market lows) tend to be sharp and with more emotion. Tops usually take longer to play out, and cannot be as easily identified.

5 | Sakata's Method and Candle Formations

Japanese history, and Japanese financial trading history, in particular, is rich with accounts of success, usually dominated by only a few individuals. One such success was a man named Munehisa (Sohkyu) Honma. Some references use Sohkyu and some use Munehisa.

Honma stepped into Japanese futures trading history in the mid-eighteenth century. When Honma was given control of the wealthy family business in 1750, he began trading at the local rice exchange in the port city of Sakata in Dewa Province, now Yamagata Prefecture, on the west coast of northern Honshu (about 220 miles north of Tokyo). Sakata was a collection and distribution port for rice and today is still one of the most important ports on the Sea of Japan.

Stories have it that Honma established a personal communications network that consisted of men on rooftops spaced every four kilometers from Osaka to Sakata. The distance between Osaka and Sakata is about 380 miles, which would have required well over 100 men. This allowed Honma the edge he needed to accumulate great wealth in rice trading.

Honma kept many records in order to learn about the psychology of investors. His studies helped him understand that the initial entry into a trade must not be rushed. According to Honma, if you feel compelled to rush into a trade because you believe that you just can't lose, wait three days to see if you still feel the same way. If you do, you can enter the trade, probably quite successfully.

The Honma family owned a great rice field near Sakata and they were considered extremely wealthy in both fact and song. One folk song said that no man can be as wealthy as a Honma: one can merely hope to be as rich as a daimyo. A daimyo is the early Japanese term for a feudal lord.

Honma died in 1803. During this period of time a book was published. "If all other people are bullish, be foolish and sell rice" is some of the advice contained in San-en Kinsen Horoku. This book was published in 1755 and is known today as the basis of Japan's market philosophy. Today, in Sakata, a house which once belonged to the Honma family, is the Honma Museum of Art.

All of the patterns and formations based upon Sakata's Method are taken from 160 rules that Honma wrote when he was 51 years old. Sakata's Method, in turn, is what is now considered as the beginnings of candle pattern recognition. Candlestick charting was not actually developed by Honma, only the pattern philosophy that goes with it. His approach has been credited as the origin of current candlestick analysis.

Since Honma came from Sakata, you may see reference to: Sakata's Law, the Sakata Method, Sakata's Five Methods, Honma Constitution, and similar names. While the labels may differ, the analysis technique remains the same. This book will refer to this approach as Sakata's Method.

Sakata's Method

Sakata's Method, as originated and used by Honma for basic chart analysis, deals with the basic yin (*inn*) and yang (*yoh*) candle lines along with two additional lines. The concept is centered around the number 3. The number 3 appears often in traditional analysis as well as in Japanese charting techniques. Sakata's Method is a technique of chart analysis using the number 3 at different points and times in the market. Sakata's Method can be summarized as:

San-zan (three mountains)
San-sen (three rivers)
San-ku (three gaps)
San-pei (three soldiers)
San-poh (three methods)

From this list it is should be obvious that san refers to the ubiquitous number 3.

San-zan (three mountains)

Three Mountains forms a line that makes a major top in the market. This is similar to the traditional Western triple top formation in which the price

Figure 5-1A

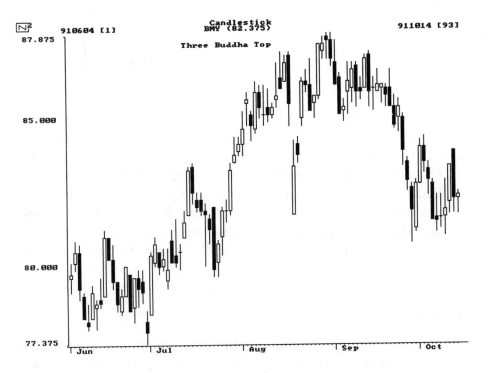

Figure 5-1B

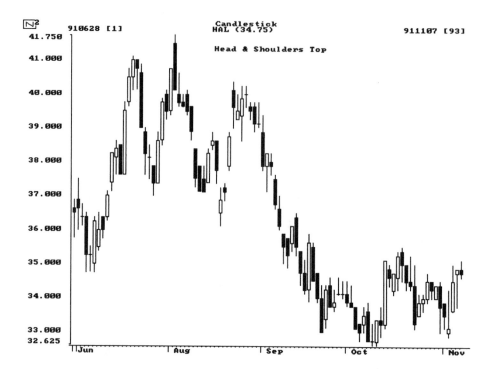

rises and falls three times, forming a top. This formation is also similar to the Three Buddha Top (*san-son*) formation which is the equivalent of the traditional head and shoulders formation. It comes from the positioning of three Buddhist images lined up, with a large Buddha in the center and a smaller one on each side. San-zan also includes the typical Western triple top where three upmoves are made with comparable corrections that follow. The three tops may be the same height or may be trending in one direction, most probably down.

San-sen (three rivers)

Three Rivers is the opposite of Three Mountains. It is often used like the traditional triple bottom or inverted head and shoulders bottom, but this is

190

Figure 5-2A

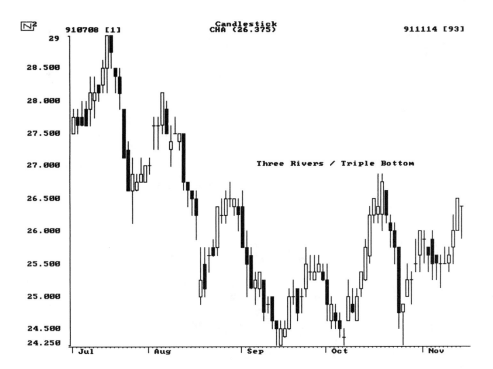

not necessarily correct. The Three Rivers method is based on the theory of using three lines to forecast the turning point of the market. This can be seen in a number of bullish candle patterns using three lines, such as the Morning Star and Three White Soldiers. In Japanese literature, the Morning Star is often called the Three Rivers Morning Star in reference to this Sakata Method.

There is some confusion about whether Sakata's Method uses Three Rivers for a bottom formation technique or whether it refers to the use of three lines for identifying tops and bottoms. There is considerable reference in Japanese literature to Three Rivers Evening Stars (a bearish pattern) and the Three Rivers Upside Gap Two Crows (also a bearish pattern). Also recall from Chapter 3 that there was a bullish reversal pattern called the Unique Three Rivers Bottom.

Figure 5-2B

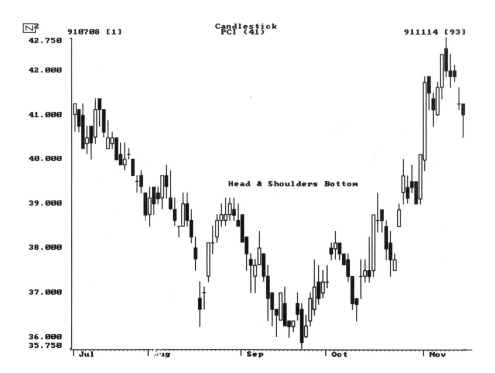

San-ku (three gaps)

This method uses gaps in price action as a means to time entry and exit points in the market. The saying goes that after a market bottom, sell on the third gap. The first gap (*ku*) demonstrates the appearance of new buying with great force. The second gap represents additional buying and possibly some covering by the sophisticated bears. The third gap is the result of short covering by the reluctant bears and any delayed market orders for buying. Here, on the third gap, Sakata's Method recommends selling because of the conflict of orders and the possibility of reaching overbought conditions too soon. This same technique works in reverse for downward gaps in the market after a top. The Japanese term for filling a gap is *anaume*. Gaps (*ku*) are also called windows (*mado*) by the Japanese.

Figure 5-3

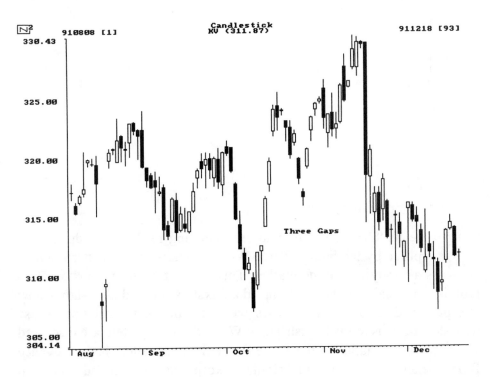

Figure 5-4

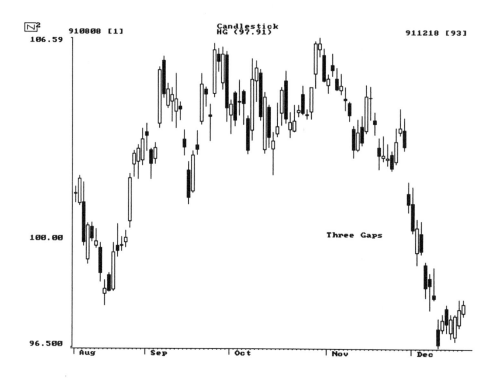

San-pei (three soldiers)

San-pei means "three soldiers who are marching in the same direction."
This is typified by the bullish Three White Soldiers candle pattern, which
indicates a steady rise in the market. This steady type of price rise shows
promise as a major move to the upside. Sakata's Method also shows how
this pattern deteriorates and shows weakness in the market rise. These
bearish variations to the bullish Three White Soldiers pattern are discussed
next. The first variation of the Three White Soldiers pattern is the Advance
Block pattern, which is quite similar, except that the second and third

white days have long upper shadows. The second variation of the Three White Soldiers pattern is the Deliberation (stalled) pattern, which also has a long upper shadow on the second day. However, the third day is a Spinning Top, and most likely a star. This suggests that a turnaround in the market is near.

Other patterns that make up the san-pei method are the Three Black Crows and the Identical Three Crows patterns. Each of these candle patterns is bearish and indicates a weak market (Chapter 3).

Figure 5-5

Figure 5-6

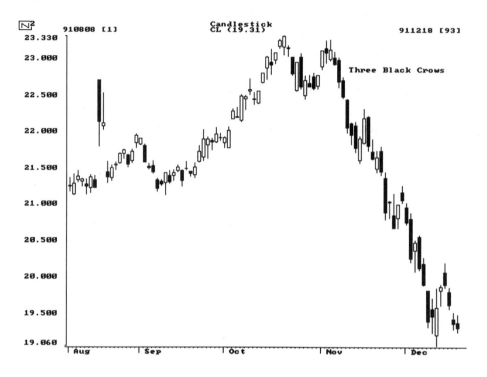

San-poh (three methods)

San-poh means "a rest or cease-fire in market action." A popular Japanese saying is "Buy, sell, and rest." Most traditional books on market psychology and trading suggest taking a break from the markets. This is necessary for many reasons, not the least of which is to get a perspective on the market while not having any money involved. San-poh involves the continuation patterns called the Rising Three Methods and the Falling Three Methods (Chapter 4). Some sources also refer to two other patterns, the Upside Gap Three Methods and Downside Gap Three Methods, all discussed in Chapter 4.

The Rising and Falling Three Methods continuation patterns are resting patterns. The trend of the market is not broken, only pausing while preparing for another advance or decline.

Sakata's Method is intended to present a clear and confident way of looking at charts. Often Sakata's Method is presented along with the following simple philosophy:

1. In an up or a down market, prices will continue to move in the established direction. This fact was instrumental in the development of candle pattern identification with a computer (Chapter 6).

2. It takes more force to cause a market to rise than to cause it to fall. This is related directly to the traditional saying that a market can fall due to its own weight.

3. A market that has risen will eventually fall, and a market that has fallen will eventually rise. As an article in the September 1991 issue of Forbes observed, in bear markets, it's smart to remind

Figure 5-7

Figure 5-8

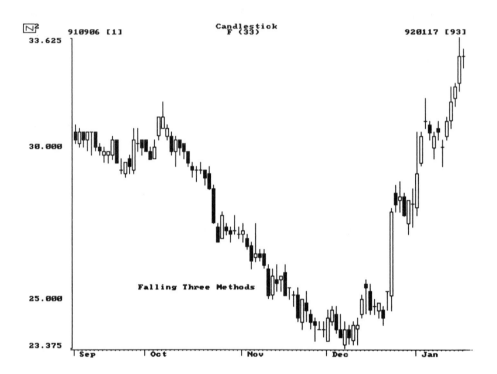

yourself that the world isn't coming to an end, and in bull markets, it's smart to remind yourself that trees don't grow to the sky. A similar and more common analogy is that all good things must come to an end.

4. Market prices sometimes just stop moving completely. This refers to lateral trading, a time for all but the most nimble traders to stand aside.

Sakata's Method, while focusing on the number 3, also involves the use of broader formations in which numerous candle patterns may exist.

Candle Formations

There are many Japanese candle formations that resemble price formations used in traditional technical analysis. Steve Nison coined many of the names commonly used in the West today. These formations can consist of many days of data. These formations are used as general market indicators and lack the precise timing that many investors and traders require. When a formation does evolve, look for additional evidence of price reversal, such as a reversal candle pattern. Some interference may occur when a formation takes shape over a long period of time. Remember that most candle patterns, and certainly almost all reversal candle patterns, require that they have a relationship with the current or previous trend. These trends are greatly influenced by the following candle formations.

Eight New Price Lines (*shinne hatte*)

Figure 5-9

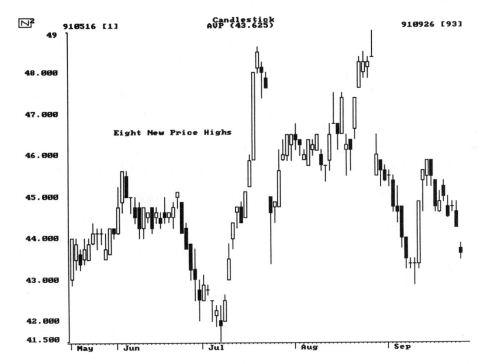

This is a formation of continually rising prices in the market. After eight new price highs are set, one should take profits, or at least protect positions with stops. Action based on ten new price highs, twelve new price highs, and thirteen new price highs is also mentioned in some literature, but not recommended here. The previous market action should be taken into consideration before using this technique.

Tweezers (*kenuki*)

Tweezers is a relatively simple formation using the components of two or more daily candle lines to determine tops and bottoms. If the high of two days is equal, the formation is called a Tweezer Top (*kenukitenjo*). Likewise, if the low of two days is equal, it is called a Tweezer Bottom (*kenukizoko*). The high or low of these days may also coincide with the open or close. This means that one day could have a long upper shadow and the next day could be an Opening Marubozu with the open (also the high) equal to the high of the previous day. The Tweezer Top or Tweezer Bottom is not limited to just two days. Days of erratic movement could occur between the two days that make up the tweezer formation.

Tweezer Tops and Tweezer Bottoms are formations that will give short term support and resistance. The terms support and resistance refer to prices that have previously turned the market. Support is a price base that stops market declines, and resistance is a level of prices that usually halts market rises. A good indication that tweezer tops and bottoms have succeeded occurs when they are also part of a reversal pattern. An example of this would be a Harami Cross in which the two highs (or lows) are equal.

Figure 5-10

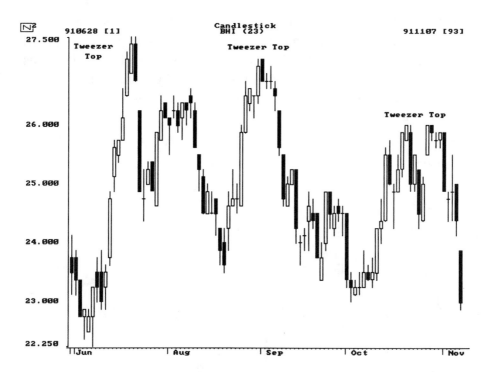

Similar in concept to the Tweezers is the Matching Low and Stick Sandwich patterns discussed in Chapter 3. These two bullish reversal patterns are derivatives of the tweezer concept, except that the close price is used exclusively, whereas the Tweezer may use any data component, such as high or low.

High Waves (*takane nochiai*)

The High Waves formation can be seen in the upper shadows on a series of candle lines. After an uptrend, a series of days such as a Shooting Star, Spinning Tops, or Gravestone Doji can produce topping tendencies. This failure to close higher shows a loss of direction and can indicate a reversal in market direction. An Advance Block pattern could also be the beginning of a High Waves formation.

Figure 5-11

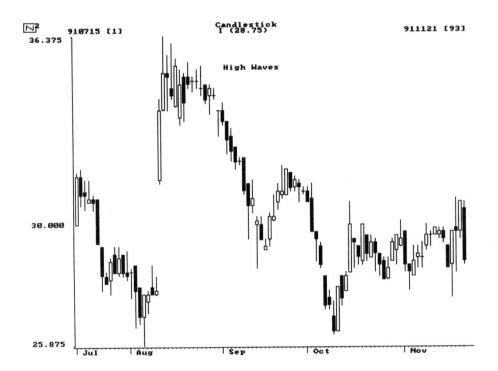

Tower Top and Tower Bottom (*ohtenjyou*)

Tower Tops and Tower Bottoms are made of many long days which slowly change color and indicate a possible reversal. Tower Bottoms occur when the market is in a downtrend, along with many long black days, but not necessarily setting significantly lower prices as in the Three Black Crows pattern. These long black days eventually become white days, and even though a turnaround isn't obvious, new closing highs are eventually made. There is nothing to say that an occasional short day cannot be part of this reversal pattern. These short days usually happen during the transition from black to white days. Of course, the Tower Top is the exact opposite. The term Tower refers to the long days which help define this pattern. Some Japanese literature refers to this type of formation as a Turret Top when it occurs at peaks.

Figure 5-12

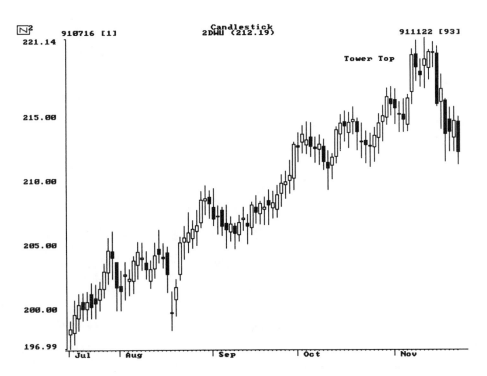

203

Figure 5-13

Fry Pan Bottom (*nabezoko*)

The Fry Pan Bottom is similar to the Tower Bottom, except that the days are all small or short body days. The bottom formation is rounded and the colors are not as important. After a number of days of slowly rounding out the bottom, a gap is made with a white day. This confirms the reversal and an uptrend should begin. The name is derived from the scooping bottom of a frying pan with a long handle.

Figure 5-14

Dumpling Top

The Dumpling Top is the counterpart of the Fry Pan Bottom formation. It is a rounded top similar to the rounded top in traditional technical jargon. The downtrend is confirmed by a gap to a black body. If the black day after the gap is a Belt Hold Line, the ability of this formation to predict future price movement is even better.

Figure 5-15

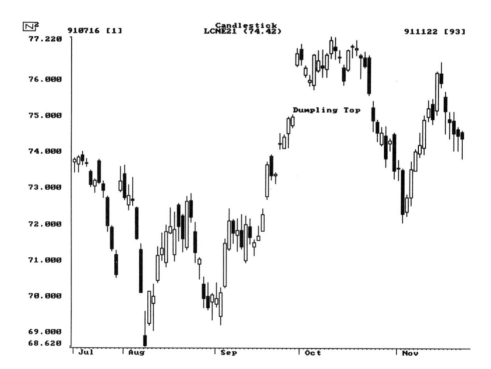

High Price Gapping Play and Low Price Gapping Play (*bohtoh* and *bohraku*)

High and Low Price Gapping Plays are the Japanese equivalents of break outs. As prices begin to consolidate near a support or resistance level, the indecision in the market becomes greater as time goes by. Once this range is broken, market direction is quickly resumed. If the break out is caused by a gap in the same direction as the prices were trending before the consolidation, a further move in that direction is certain. Because of the subjective nature of these formations, the textbook cases will rarely be seen. Basically, they are the same as the Rising and Falling Three Methods and the Mat Hold, except that no clear arrangement of candlesticks can be used to define them.

Figure 5-16

Figure 5-17

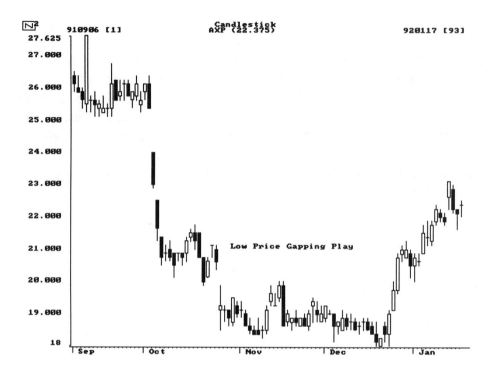

6 | The Philosophy Behind Candle Pattern Identification

Data Requirements, Gaps, and Rules

Only daily price data, which consists of open, high, low, and close prices on a stock or commodity, is being used when explaining these concepts. Many times, the open price is not available on stocks. In such cases the previous day's closing price has been substituted. The exception to this is when the previous day's close is higher than today's high, today's high is used for the open. Similarly, when the previous day's close is lower than today's low, today's low is used as the open price. This allows the visibility of gaps from one day's close to the next day's range.

Gaps are an important part of candlestick analysis. To demonstrate that there is not much difference, the S&P 100 stocks with and without open price were tested and analyzed. Comprehensive testing was also accomplished on vast amounts of data that contained the open price to see if there was any statistical information about gaps that could be used when the open price was not available. Whenever a day's high and low prices were greater than the high price of the preceding day, a gap-up analysis was performed. Likewise, whenever a day's high and low price were less than the previous day's low price, a gap-down analysis was done. Once a "gap day" was identified, the following formula was used to determine the location of the open price relative to the day's range:

$$[(Open - Low) / (High - Low)] * 100$$

The results showed consistently that the open price was 17 to 31 percent into the high-low range following a gap. If the gap was to the upside, the open price would fall about 17 to 28 percent above the low price. Similarly, if the gap was to the downside, the open price would fall 17 to 31 percent below the high price. Remember, these are just statistics calculated from a large amount of data, so the usual precautions are suggested.

Figure 6-1

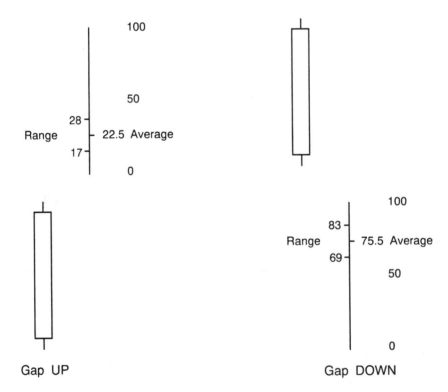

One must also be aware that certain candle patterns cannot exist if there is no open price. That is, the previous day's close cannot be substituted for the open. The following candle patterns cannot exist when the open price is not available.

- **Inverted Hammer**

- **Dark Cloud Cover**

- **Piercing Line**

- **Meeting Lines**

- **Upside Gap Two Crows**

- **Two Crows**

- **Unique Three River Bottom**

- **Kicking**

- **Matching Low**

- **Side-by-Side White Lines**

- **Three Line Strike**

- **In Neck Line**

There are techniques that can be used in computerized candle pattern identification that will still allow these patterns to be used. For example, one could set some parameters that relate the data components from "greater than" to "greater than or equal to." As a result a requirement that the open of one day to be less than the close of the previous day could be modified so that the open could also be equal. Although this may stretch the philosophy of candle pattern recognition too far, it at least permits the use of data that do not contain the open price.

Today's electronic capabilities let traders watch intraday price movements from single trade ticks, one minute bars, and almost any other conceivable increment in between. It is not the purpose here to decide which type is better, but sometimes the trees do get in the way of the forest. One must also keep in mind that candle patterns reflect the short term psychology of trading, including the decision process that occurs after a market is closed. This is why open and close prices are so important.

Using intraday day data without the benefit of a break is questionable at the very least.

The Idea

Pattern recognition has been around for many years. A computer can check and scan vast amounts of data and compile unlimited statistics on patterns and their ability to forecast prices. This approach never remains popular for very long because it is based solely on statistics and overlooks an important explanation of why some patterns are more successful than others—human psychology.

Enter Human Psychology

In the first few minutes of the trading day, a great deal of overnight emotion is captured. Sometimes special events will even cause chaos. For example, on the New York Exchange, it may take several minutes for the specialists to open a stock for trading because of a large order imbalance. However, once a stock or commodity does open, a point of reference has been established. From this reference point, trading decisions are made throughout the day.

As the trading day progresses, extremes are reached as speculator emotion is tossed around. These extremes of emotion are recorded as the high and low of the trading day. Finally, the trading day ends and the last trade is recorded as the closing price. This is the price that many will use to help make decisions about their positions and the tactics they will use at the open of the next trading day.

Aside from intraday data, four prices are normally available for the trader to analyze. One certainly knows the exact open and close prices for any trading day, but at what times during the day the high and low were reached, and in what order, are not known.

How does one determine the existence of a candlestick pattern?

Most candle patterns require the identification of, not only the data relationship making the pattern, but also the trend immediately preceding the pattern. The trend is what sets up the psychology of traders for the candle pattern to develop. Most of the current literature somehow evades this essential ingredient to candle pattern recognition.

It must also be stated here that Japanese candlestick analysis is short term (one to ten days) analysis. Any patterns that give longer term results are surely just coincidental.

Trend Determination

What is a trend? This question, if it could be answered in depth, could reveal the secrets of the marketplace and maybe even the universe. For this discussion, only a simple and highly reliable short term answer is sought.

Trend analysis is a primary part of technical analysis. To some, trend identification is as important as the timing of reversal points in the market. Technical analysis books deal with the subject of trend quite thoroughly and define it in numerous ways. One of the most common approaches is the moving average.

Moving Averages and Smoothing

One of the simplest market systems created, the moving average, works almost as well as the best of the complicated smoothing techniques. A moving average is exactly the same as a regular average except that it "moves" because it is continuously updated as new data become available. Each data point in a moving average is given equal weight in the computation, hence the term arithmetic or simple is sometimes used when referring to a moving average.

A moving average smooths a sequence of numbers so that the effects of short term fluctuations are reduced, while those of longer term fluctuations remain relatively unchanged. Obviously, the time span of the moving average will alter its characteristics.

J. M. Hurst in *The Profit Magic of Stock Transaction Timing* (1970) explained these alterations with three general rules:

1. A moving average of any given time span exactly reduces the magnitude of the fluctuations of duration equal to that time span to zero.

2. The same moving average also greatly reduces (but does not eliminate) the magnitude of all fluctuations of duration less than the time span of the moving average.

3. All fluctuations are greater than the time span of the average "come through," or are also present in the resulting moving average line. Those with durations just a little greater than the span of the average are greatly reduced in magnitude, but the effect lessens as periodicity duration increases. Very long duration periodicities come through nearly unscathed.

A somewhat more advanced smoothing technique is the exponential moving average. In principle, it accomplishes the same thing as the simple (arithmetic) moving average. Exponential smoothing was developed to assist in radar tracking and flight path projection. A quicker projection of trend was needed with more influence from the most recent data. The formula for exponential smoothing appears complex, but it is only another way of weighting the data components so that the most recent data receive the greatest weight. Even though only two data points are required to get an exponentially smoothed value, the more data used the better. All of the data are used and are a part of the new result.

A simple explanation of exponential smoothing is therefore given here. An exponential average utilizes a smoothing constant that approximates the number of days for a simple moving average. This constant is multiplied by the difference between today's closing price and the previous day's moving average value. This new value is then added to the previous day's moving average value. The smoothing constant is equivalent to $2/(n+1)$ where n is the number of days used for a simple moving average.

The Trend Method Used

After conducting numerous tests, a short term exponential smoothing of the data was determined to best identify the short term trend. It gives the best, easiest, and quickest determination of the short term trend and is certainly a concept which one can understand. Simple concepts are usually more reliable and certainly more creditable.

Numerous tests were performed on vast amounts of data with the finding that a exponential period of ten days seemed to work as well as any, especially when you recall that candlesticks have a short term orientation.

Identifying the Candle Patterns

Previous chapters presented detailed descriptions of the exact relationships among the open, high, low, and close. Those chapters also dealt with the concept of trend use, while this chapter focused on trend determination. In addition, a method of determining long days, short days, doji days, etc. is needed, including the relationship between the body and the shadows. The latter is essential for proper identification of patterns such as the Hanging Man and Hammer. The following sections will show the multitude of methods used to accomplish these and similar tasks.

Long Days

Any of three different methods are available, where each, or any combination, of the three can be used to determine long days. The term minimum in these formulas refers to the minimum acceptable percentage for a long day. Any day whose body is greater than this minimum value will be considered a long day.

1. Long Body / Price – Minimum (0 to 100%)

    This method will relate the day in question with the actual value of the prices for a stock or commodity. If the value is set at 5% and the price is at 100, then a long day will be any day whose range from open to close is 5 points or more. This method does not use any past data to determine a long day.

2. Long Body / High to Low Range – Minimum (0 to 100%)

This method uses the body length in relation to the high-low range for a given day under this technique. If a candle does not have long shadows, it is considered a long day. Used by itself, this is not the best method; used in conjunction with one or both of the other methods, it is good. This method will eliminate days that might appear more as Spinning Tops when viewed with the surrounding data.

3. Long Body / Average Body of Last X days – Minimum (0 to 100%)

An average of the body sizes of the last X days is used to determine a long body. The value for X should be anywhere between five and ten days. If the percentage was set to 130, then a long day would be identified if it was 30% greater than this average. This method is good because it falls in line with the general concept of candlesticks and their use for short term analysis.

Short Days

The exact same concept for determining long days is used for short days with one exception: instead of minimum percentages, maximum percentages are used in the three formulas.

Small Body / Large Body Relationship

The Engulfing Pattern and Harami use both a large body and a small body for their patterns. This large body and small body concept is not the same as the long body and short body concept discussed previously. Here the large and small bodies refer only to their relationship with one another. One must decide how much engulfing constitutes an Engulfing Pattern. If the concept is held to the letter of the law, then only one tick or minimum price movement is required to cause an engulfment. Can this be at just one end of the body when the prices are equal at the other end? In other words, can the open-to-close range be different by only one tick? The following formula will let you control this situation.

Small Body / Large Body – Maximum (0 to 100%)

The inverse of this value can be used for the Harami. It is recommended to use values that represent what could easily be identified if the determination were made visually. If a small body is engulfed by a large body by 70%, it means that the small body cannot exceed 70% of the size of the large body. Said another way, the large body is approximately 30% larger than the small body.

Umbrella Days

Remember, an umbrella day occurs when the body is at the upper end of the day's range and the lower shadow is considerably longer than the body. One must also take into consideration the length of the upper shadow, if one exists. The body and lower shadow relationship is defined as a percentage of body length to lower shadow length:

Umbrella Body / Lower Shadow (0 to 100%)

If this value is set to 50, then the body cannot exceed 50% of the size of the lower shadow. In this example, the lower shadow would be at least twice the length of the body. The upper shadow on an umbrella day can be handled in a similar fashion, such as:

Umbrella Upper Shadow / High to Low Range (0 to 100%)

The upper shadow is related to the entire day's range. A value of 10 means that the upper shadow is only 10% (or less) of the high-low range. These variables will help identify the Hanging Man and Hammer candle patterns. Patterns such as the Shooting Star and Inverted Hammer use just the inverse of these settings.

Doji Days

Doji occurs when the open and close prices are equal. This is an exceptionally restrictive rule for most types of data and should have some leeway when identifying candle patterns. The formula lets you set a percentage difference between the two prices that will be acceptable.

Doji Body / High to Low Range – Maximum (0 to 100%)

This value is a percentage maximum of the prices relative to the range of prices on the Doji day. A value in the neighborhood of 1 to 3% seems to work quite well.

Equal Values

Equal values occur when prices are required to be equal. This is used for patterns like Meeting Lines and Separating Lines. Meeting Lines require that the close price of each day be equal; while Separating Lines require the open prices to be equal. The same concept used in determining a Doji day can be used here as well. There are a few instances when setting the parameters to the literal definition will restrict, rather than enhance, the pattern concept.

Computerized Analysis and Anomalies

The candle pattern statistics in Table 6-1 shows the amount of data used in this analysis, the type of data used, and various other pertinent statistics. Data were obtained from stocks with and without open price, CSI's perpetual futures contracts, and leading market indexes.

A total pattern frequency of slightly less than 11% equates to one candle pattern about every nine trading days. This represents a good frequency for daily analysis of stocks and futures. Reversal patterns occur

Table 6-1

Candle Pattern Statistics - 920331

	Stocks w/ OPEN	Stocks w/o OPEN	Futures	Indices	TOTALS	Percent of TOTAL
Total Issues	243	1416	41	13	1713	
Total Data Records	113472	896290	49307	6940	1066009	

Reversal Patterns

Hammer+	1817	20493	174	53	22537	2.114%
Hanging Man-	1721	13866	163	126	15876	1.489%
Engulfing+	1218	12166	451	86	13921	1.306%
Engulfing-	988	10284	453	84	11809	1.108%
Harami+	989	11569	442	92	13092	1.228%
Harami-	1643	15470	467	150	17730	1.663%
Harami Cross+	364	276	24	3	667	0.063%
Harami Cross-	485	364	30	4	883	0.083%
Inverted Hammer+	137	0	31	0	168	0.016%
Shooting Star-	66	600	5	1	672	0.063%
Piercing Line+	136	0	111	3	250	0.023%
Dark Cloud Cover-	144	0	122	3	269	0.025%
Doji Star+	265	582	21	2	870	0.082%
Doji Star-	293	480	37	4	814	0.076%
Morning Star+	32	78	25	0	135	0.013%
Evening Star-	30	83	32	1	146	0.014%
Morning Doji Star+	33	41	14	3	91	0.009%
Evening Doji Star-	15	4	10	0	29	0.003%
Abandoned Baby+	0	13	4	0	17	0.002%
Abandoned Baby-	0	16	2	0	18	0.002%
Tri-Star+	31	151	0	1	183	0.017%
Tri-Star-	31	158	0	9	198	0.019%
Upside Gap Two Crows-	3	0	18	0	21	0.002%
Meeting Lines+	2	0	3	0	5	0.000%
Meeting Lines-	25	0	8	1	34	0.003%
Belt Hold+	242	863	17	3	1125	0.106%
Belt Hold-	294	1124	22	22	1462	0.137%
Unique Three River+	0	0	1	0	1	0.000%
Three White Soldiers+	26	71	4	4	105	0.010%
Deliberation-	51	118	20	3	192	0.018%
Advance Block-	23	212	1	2	238	0.022%
Three Black Crows-	19	10	12	1	42	0.004%
Identical Three Crows-	9	295	1	3	308	0.029%
Breakaway+	1	33	4	0	38	0.004%
Breakaway-	1	34	4	0	39	0.004%
Two Crows-	18	0	24	0	42	0.004%
Three Inside Up+	82	695	46	12	835	0.078%
Three Inside Down-	103	711	49	7	870	0.082%
Three Outside Up+	289	2713	131	31	3164	0.297%
Three Outside Down-	238	1964	128	18	2348	0.220%
Three Stars in the South+	1	6	0	0	7	0.001%
Concealing Baby Swallow+	0	0	1	0	1	0.000%
Stick Sandwich+	1	49	2	0	52	0.005%
Kicking+	0	0	0	0	0	0.000%
Kicking-	0	0	1	0	1	0.000%
Homing Pigeon+	36	947	24	0	1007	0.094%
Ladder Bottom+	6	98	0	0	104	0.010%
Matching Low+	67	0	4	0	71	0.007%
Reversal TOTALS	11975	96637	3143	732	112487	10.552%

Table 6-1 (continued)

Continuation Patterns	Stocks w/ OPEN	Stocks w/o OPEN	Futures	Indices	TOTALS	Percent of TOTAL
Upside Tasuki Gap+	66	286	88	3	443	0.042%
Downside Tasuki Gap-	35	327	90	4	456	0.043%
Side by Side White Lines+	23	0	4	0	27	0.003%
Side by Side White Lines-	2	0	4	0	6	0.001%
Rising Three Methods+	65	445	13	8	531	0.050%
Falling Three Methods-	10	249	17	5	281	0.026%
Separating Lines+	21	53	5	0	79	0.007%
Separating Lines-	23	57	3	0	83	0.008%
Three Line Strike+	26	0	16	1	43	0.004%
Three Line Strike-	21	0	17	1	39	0.004%
UPside Gap Three Methods+	32	207	10	0	249	0.023%
DNside Gap Three Methods-	17	185	22	0	224	0.021%
On Neck Line-	96	515	43	0	654	0.061%
In Neck Line-	153	0	58	0	211	0.020%
Continuation TOTALS	590	2324	390	22	3326	0.312%
TOTAL (ALL Patterns)	12565	98961	3533	754	115813	10.864%

about 30 times more often than continuation patterns. This too is important, as it indicates the reversal of a trend caused by changed positions in trading. In this analysis, there were 48 reversal patterns and 14 continuation patterns, which makes reversal patterns account for about 77% of all patterns.

It is also interesting to note that 6 patterns account for almost 9% of all patterns. Of this, the Harami pattern accounts for 32% of those 6 patterns and almost 3% of all patterns. Finally, please note that some patterns occurred quite infrequently. To assess whether or not they have any value, you should refer to the scoring statistics in Chapter 7. When a pattern occurs, you must understand that, statistically, the success or failure does not mean much. Success and/or failure of candle patterns is dealt with extensively in Chapter 7.

When a particular pattern appears only a few times in a large amount of data, you should realize that its success and/or failure is subject to the time period under study. Do not let statistics interfere with common sense, and certainly be alert for inaccuracies in the data.

Remember, candle patterns were used as a visual charting technique for hundreds of years. With computers there is no way to handle the subjectivity that classic chart reading offers. Another factor to consider when using computers is the quality of the graphics screen: its resolution. The screen consists of small dots of light known as pixel elements. If too much data is used, or if the range of the data is too great, then what might appear as equal on the screen would not be so numerically. The smallest size (width) horizontal line could have a price range within itself, not visible to the eye. Not only computer screens, but also computer generated chart books could have this problem. This is why some flexibility must be built into the identification of, and definition of, the classic patterns.

Another computer anomaly arises in handling candle patterns that are within, or part of, another candle pattern. A computer will look at the data in chronological order, that is, old data first. As each day is added, a candle pattern may or may not be noted. When a pattern is identified, the results are stored and the process continues. If a bullish Engulfing Day is identified and the next day has a white body with a close greater than the first day of the Engulfing Day, a Three Outside Up pattern is noted and recorded. The data for statistics and testing has been acquired for both patterns. However, only the Three Outside Up pattern will be identified as a candle pattern if it is given higher priority.

7 | Reliability of Pattern Recognition

Using the identification philosophy developed in the previous chapter, one can now adapt a method of determining just how successful candle patterns are.

Measures of Success

The following three assumptions were used in measuring the success and/or failure of the many different candle patterns:

1. The pattern must, of course, be identified based upon its open, high, low, and close relationships.

2. For the pattern to be identified, the trend must be determined. This is interchangeable with the previous assumption; each must exist in the methodology.

3. Some basis of measurement must be established to determine the success or failure of the candle pattern.

To make a creditable prediction, you either know the current trend or you do not. Both assumptions and possibilities have been used here.

The Trend Is Known

Candle patterns fall into two general categories: those that indicate a reversal of the current trend and those that indicate trend continuation.

Each day (for each tradeable), a prediction is made about whether the known trend will continue or reverse for each prediction interval. In other words, if today's close is above the exponential average (trend), then we assume that we are in an uptrend. The success or failure is measured by the change in this trend over the prediction interval. The prediction interval is the number of days into the future the success or failure was based upon. Prediction intervals refer to the time periods between the actual candle pattern and some point in the future.

When a candle pattern occurs, it is offering a short-term forecast on the direction of the underlying market. The prediction interval is the number of days after the candle pattern that a determination is made as to whether or not the candle pattern was successful. A prediction interval is a time in the future that measures the candle pattern's forecasting ability.

Once a trend starts, the odds are that it will continue. Every student of science or engineering will recognize that this is nothing more than Newton's First Law of Motion, which says, Every body continues in a state of rest or of uniform motion in a straight line unless it is compelled to change that state by forces applied to it. Simply said, it is easier for a market to continue its direction than to reverse its direction.

Therefore, the continuation of a trend is more common than the reversal of a trend. Remember, we are talking about the short-term future here.

If, at the prediction interval, the price is still above the trend, then the candle pattern was successful. Simply said: If, during the prediction interval, we are still in an uptrend, then it was deemed successful (Figure 7-1). If not, it was a failure. Figure 7-1 graphically shows the relationship of reversal and continuation patterns with the prediction interval. The relationship of pattern type with prediction interval is based upon the fact that the trend is known.

Figure 7-1

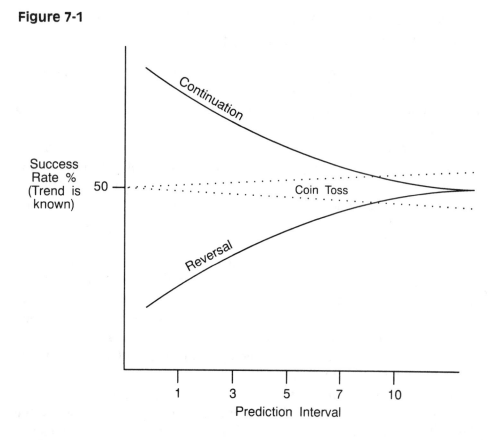

The Trend Is Not Known

Sometimes you do not know what the trend is before making the prediction. In such cases, a coin-toss type of prediction is made about whether the price will go up or down. If you do not know the trend, the odds of its continuing or reversing would fall into the area of 50%. The difference above or below 50% would reflect the directional bias of the data used in the analysis. Again, the success or failure is based upon the price at the prediction interval relative to the change in trend. This fact is also shown in Figure 7-1. Remember, most candle patterns require that the trend be identified.

Reverse Current Trend
and Continue Current Trend

From the computer calculations, two primary parameters are determined: Reverse Current Trend and Continue Current Trend. These are further broken down into Up and Down trends (i.e., Reverse Current Trend Up and Reverse Current Trend Down).

The sum of Reverse Current Trend success and Continue Current Trend success will be equal to the number of days of data used in the testing process. Since a prediction is made each day, Reverse Current Trend success and Continue Current Trend failure would be equal. In other words, the success of Reverse Current Trend, is also the failure of Continue Current Trend.

Reversal candle patterns (which most are) are compared to Reverse Current Trend and further broken down into upturns and downturns. Since reversal candle patterns must go against the very trend that defines them, their measure of success would not be as rigid as that of a continuation candle pattern. In fact, their measure of success could actually be less than that of a coin toss, since they are predicting a change in the current trend, a trend which is supposedly known.

Likewise, continuation candle patterns are compared to Continue Current Trend. Continuation candle patterns say that the trend that helped define them is going to continue. Therefore, for a continuation candle pattern to be considered successful, it must do better than the success of knowing the trend in the first place. Because we know the current trend and we know that the odds are that the current trend will continue; to be useful, continuation patterns must be exceptionally good, or are no better than the trend-identification process.

Candle Pattern Statistical Ranking

Candle patterns are predictable psychological trading pictures (windows) that produce reasonable forecasting results when used in the proper manner. This section will explain the technique used to determine the various statistics developed to show the success of candle patterns. Note that no magnitude of success is used, only relative success and failure. Keep in mind, though, that success still means that the pattern correctly predicted the market move and failure means that it did not.

Using all of the information about pattern recognition (including trend determination) developed in the previous chapters, we will now set out to see just how good candle patterns are. Because a simple approach is usually best, no elaborate assumptions were used, only the price change over various time intervals into the future.

Once the relative success or failure of a particular candle pattern was determined, its relationship to the appropriate pattern standard of measure was calculated. This standard of measure is the Reverse Current Trend and Continue Current Trend, discussed earlier. Recall that continuation patterns must outperform reversal patterns because of their trend relationship. That is why you will see many continuation patterns with a negative ranking, even though their success percentage was high.

Candle Patterns and Stocks

Data for this analysis were the stocks contained in the Standard and Poor's 100 Index and 41 futures contracts. The S&P 100 Index is a capitalization-weighted index of 100 stocks from a broad range of industries. These 100 stocks present an excellent representation of the U.S. stock market. The futures contracts used were perpetual contracts from CSI (Commodity Systems, Inc). These contracts were used so that long-term continuous data could be analyzed.

The results, presented in Tables 7-1 through 7-3, use prediction intervals of three, five, and seven days. This should adequately cover the time interval used when doing candle pattern analysis. When prediction intervals from one to ten days are analyzed the results from all ten fall within the expected range represented with these tables.

Table 7-1 presents the results of the candle pattern ranking system for a prediction interval of three days, using over 82,000 days of data. Notice that 55 of the 62 possible patterns occurred in the 100 stocks used in this test, but that a few were somewhat sparse. About 65% (36 out of 55) of the

Table 7-1

CANDLE PATTERN RANKING
Interval: 3   100 Autoruns/C:\n2\sp100\   Periods: 821

Rankings Based on Percent Improvement Over RANDOM Calls

No.	Type	Name	Total	Success	%Success	%Ranking
1	R-	Identical 3 Crows-	8	8	100.00	230.03
2	R+	Three White Soldiers+	19	17	89.40	170.09
3	R-	Three Black Crows-	17	13	76.40	152.15
4	R-	Three Inside Down-	76	52	68.40	125.74
5	R-	Three Outside Down-	175	118	67.40	122.44
6	R-	Upside Gap Two Crows-	3	2	66.60	119.80
7	R+	Three Outside Up+	208	139	66.80	101.81
8	R+	Three Inside Up+	59	37	62.70	89.43
9	R-	Engulfing Pattern-	694	356	51.20	68.98
10	R+	Engulfing Pattern+	908	500	55.00	66.16
11	R+	Morning Doji Star+	25	13	52.00	57.10
12	R+	Tri-Star+	18	9	50.00	51.06
13	C	Falling Three Methods-	5	5	100.00	49.48
14	R+	Piercing Line+	100	48	48.00	45.02
15	R-	Dark Cloud Cover-	107	47	43.90	44.88
16	R+	Morning Star+	21	10	47.60	43.81
17	R-	Belt Hold-	202	86	42.50	40.26
18	R+	Homing Pigeon+	22	10	45.40	37.16
19	C	Side/Side White Lines+	16	15	93.70	34.43
20	R-	Evening Star-	23	9	39.10	29.04
21	R-	Two Crows-	13	5	38.40	26.73
22	R+	Belt Hold+	190	79	41.50	25.38
23	C	Separating Lines-	12	10	83.30	24.51
24	C	Separating Lines+	11	9	81.80	17.36
25	C	Upside Tasuki Gap+	49	40	81.60	17.07
26	R-	Tri-Star-	15	5	33.30	9.90
27	R-	Evening Doji Star-	9	3	33.30	9.90
28	C	On Neck Line-	78	57	73.00	9.12
29	R+	Harami Cross+	277	99	35.70	7.85
30	R+	Inverted Hammer+	109	38	34.80	5.14
31	C	In Neck Line-	118	83	70.30	5.08
32	R+	Harami+	755	261	34.50	4.23
33	C	Rising Three Methods+	43	31	72.00	3.30
34	R-	Harami-	1165	358	30.70	1.32
35	R-	Hanging Man-	1175	361	30.70	1.32
36	R+	Hammer+	1336	447	33.40	0.91
37	R-	Harami Cross-	340	99	29.10	-3.96
38	C	Downside Tasuki Gap-	29	18	62.00	-7.32
39	C	DNside Gap 3 Methods-	13	8	61.50	-8.07
40	C	UPside Gap 3 Methods+	24	15	62.50	-10.33
41	C	Three Line Strike-	16	9	56.20	-15.99
42	R-	Shooting Star-	36	9	25.00	-17.49
43	R+	Doji Star+	178	44	24.70	-25.38
44	R+	Matching Low+	42	9	21.40	-35.35
45	R+	Ladder Bottom+	5	1	20.00	-39.58
46	R-	Deliberation-	30	5	16.60	-45.21
47	C	Three Line Strike+	19	7	36.80	-47.20
48	R-	Doji Star-	157	24	15.20	-49.83
49	R-	Advance Block-	17	1	5.80	-80.86
50	R+	Meeting Lines+	2	0	0.00	-100.00
51	R-	Meeting Lines-	10	0	0.00	-100.00
52	R+	Stick Sandwich+	1	0	0.00	-100.00
53	R+	3 Stars in the South+	1	0	0.00	-100.00
54	C	Side/Side White Lines-	1	0	0.00	-100.00
55	R+	Breakaway+	1	0	0.00	-100.00

Table 7-2

```
                        CANDLE PATTERN RANKING
        Interval: 5       100 Autoruns/C:\n2\sp100\       Periods: 821

        Rankings Based on Percent Improvement Over RANDOM Calls
```

No.	Type	Name	Total	Success	%Success	%Ranking
1	R+	Three White Soldiers+	19	16	84.20	108.93
2	R-	Three Black Crows-	17	13	76.40	107.05
3	R-	Upside Gap Two Crows-	3	2	66.60	80.49
4	R-	Three Outside Down-	174	109	62.60	69.65
5	R-	Identical 3 Crows-	8	5	62.50	69.38
6	R+	Morning Doji Star+	25	16	64.00	58.81
7	R-	Evening Star-	23	13	56.50	53.12
8	R+	Three Outside Up+	208	124	59.60	47.89
9	C	Separating Lines+	11	10	90.90	44.06
10	R-	Three Inside Down-	76	40	52.60	42.55
11	R-	Engulfing Pattern-	692	353	51.00	38.21
12	R-	Dark Cloud Cover-	107	51	47.60	29.00
13	R+	Three Inside Up+	59	30	50.80	26.05
14	R+	Meeting Lines+	2	1	50.00	24.07
15	R+	Homing Pigeon+	22	11	50.00	24.07
16	R+	Engulfing Pattern+	907	446	49.10	21.84
17	R+	Piercing Line+	100	48	48.00	19.11
18	R-	Belt Hold-	201	88	43.70	18.43
19	C	Rising Three Methods+	43	32	74.40	17.91
20	C	DNside Gap 3 Methods-	13	9	69.20	15.91
21	R+	Harami Cross+	277	126	45.40	12.66
22	C	Separating Lines-	12	8	66.60	11.56
23	C	Upside Tasuki Gap+	49	34	69.30	9.83
24	C	On Neck Line-	78	51	65.30	9.38
25	R+	Harami+	751	326	43.40	7.69
26	R+	Belt Hold+	189	78	41.20	2.23
27	R-	Hanging Man-	1171	436	37.20	0.81
28	C	Three Line Strike+	19	12	63.10	0.00
29	R+	Ladder Bottom+	5	2	40.00	-0.74
30	R-	Harami-	1164	423	36.30	-1.63
31	R+	Matching Low+	41	16	39.00	-3.23
32	R+	Tri-Star+	18	7	38.80	-3.72
33	R+	Hammer+	1334	514	38.50	-4.47
34	C	In Neck Line-	118	67	56.70	-5.03
35	R+	Morning Star+	21	8	38.00	-5.71
36	R-	Harami Cross-	340	115	33.80	-8.40
37	R-	Tri-Star-	15	5	33.30	-9.76
38	R-	Shooting Star-	36	12	33.30	-9.76
39	R+	Inverted Hammer+	109	38	34.80	-13.65
40	C	UPside Gap 3 Methods+	24	13	54.10	-14.26
41	C	Three Line Strike-	16	8	50.00	-16.25
42	R-	Two Crows-	13	4	30.70	-16.80
43	C	Downside Tasuki Gap-	29	14	48.20	-19.26
44	C	Side/Side White Lines+	16	8	50.00	-20.76
45	R+	Doji Star+	178	53	29.70	-26.30
46	C	Falling Three Methods-	5	2	40.00	-33.00
47	R-	Deliberation-	30	7	23.30	-36.86
48	R-	Evening Doji Star-	9	2	22.20	-39.84
49	R-	Doji Star-	154	33	21.40	-42.01
50	R-	Advance Block-	17	2	11.70	-68.29
51	R-	Meeting Lines-	10	1	10.00	-72.90
52	R+	Stick Sandwich+	1	0	0.00	-100.00
53	C	Side/Side White Lines-	1	0	0.00	-100.00
54	R+	3 Stars in the South+	1	0	0.00	-100.00
55	R+	Breakaway+	1	0	0.00	-100.00

Table 7-3

CANDLE PATTERN RANKING
Interval: 7   100 Autoruns/C:\n2\sp100\   Periods: 821

Rankings Based on Percent Improvement Over RANDOM Calls

No.	Type	Name	Total	Success	%Success	%Ranking
1	R+	Stick Sandwich+	1	1	100.00	123.21
2	R+	Meeting Lines+	2	2	100.00	123.21
3	R-	Three Black Crows-	17	11	64.70	57.42
4	R+	Three White Soldiers+	19	11	57.80	29.02
5	R-	Advance Block-	17	9	52.90	28.71
6	R+	Three Inside Up+	59	34	57.60	28.57
7	R-	Shooting Star-	36	19	52.70	28.22
8	R-	Three Outside Down-	172	88	51.10	24.33
9	C	Separating Lines+	11	8	72.70	23.43
10	R-	Meeting Lines-	10	5	50.00	21.65
11	C	Upside Tasuki Gap+	49	35	71.40	21.22
12	C	On Neck Line-	78	52	66.60	20.65
13	C	Separating Lines-	12	8	66.60	20.65
14	R-	Dark Cloud Cover-	107	52	48.50	18.00
15	R+	Three Outside Up+	208	109	52.40	16.96
16	C	Three Line Strike+	19	13	68.40	16.13
17	R+	Morning Doji Star+	25	13	52.00	16.07
18	R-	Three Inside Down-	76	36	47.30	15.09
19	R+	Piercing Line+	100	51	51.00	13.84
20	C	Rising Three Methods+	42	28	66.60	13.07
21	C	UPside Gap 3 Methods+	24	16	66.60	13.07
22	R-	Engulfing Pattern-	689	319	46.20	12.41
23	R+	Homing Pigeon+	22	11	50.00	11.61
24	R+	Matching Low+	41	20	48.70	8.71
25	C	Falling Three Methods-	5	3	60.00	8.70
26	R+	Morning Star+	21	10	47.60	6.25
27	C	Downside Tasuki Gap-	29	17	58.60	6.16
28	R+	Harami+	750	356	47.40	5.80
29	R+	Engulfing Pattern+	907	429	47.20	5.36
30	R-	Harami-	1157	501	43.30	5.35
31	R-	Deliberation-	30	13	43.30	5.35
32	R-	Belt Hold-	199	86	43.20	5.11
33	R+	Harami Cross+	277	130	46.90	4.69
34	R-	Hanging Man-	1166	497	42.60	3.65
35	R+	Belt Hold+	189	87	46.00	2.68
36	R+	Hammer+	1331	591	44.40	-0.89
37	C	DNside Gap 3 Methods-	13	7	53.80	-2.54
38	R-	Tri-Star-	15	6	40.00	-2.68
39	C	Side/Side White Lines+	16	9	56.20	-4.58
40	R-	Harami Cross-	340	133	39.10	-4.87
41	R-	Evening Star-	23	9	39.10	-4.87
42	C	Three Line Strike-	16	8	50.00	-9.42
43	C	In Neck Line-	118	58	49.10	-11.05
44	R-	Upside Gap Two Crows-	3	1	33.30	-18.98
45	R-	Evening Doji Star-	9	3	33.30	-18.98
46	R+	Inverted Hammer+	109	38	34.80	-22.32
47	R-	Doji Star-	154	49	31.80	-22.63
48	R+	Doji Star+	178	61	34.20	-23.66
49	R+	Tri-Star+	18	6	33.30	-25.67
50	R-	Identical 3 Crows-	8	2	25.00	-39.17
51	R-	Two Crows-	13	3	23.00	-44.04
52	R+	Ladder Bottom+	5	1	20.00	-55.36
53	R+	3 Stars in the South+	1	0	0.00	-100.00
54	C	Side/Side White Lines-	1	0	0.00	-100.00
55	R+	Breakaway+	1	0	0.00	-100.00

candle patterns were deemed successful using the established ranking criteria.

The data offer a good example of the difference in importance between reversal patterns and continuation patterns. The reversal pattern Identical Three Crows had a 100% success and a ranking score of 230.03%. The continuation pattern Falling Three Methods also had a 100% success, but its ranking score was only 49.48%. The difference in ranking scores occurs because continuation patterns only suggest that the known trend will continue, which, of course, is favored by the odds. In contrast, reversal patterns indicate that the trend will reverse, which is less likely to occur.

As Table 7-2 shows, using a prediction interval of five days decreased the number of successful patterns somewhat. Only 28 out of 55 patterns were ranked as successful, or just a little over 50%. Notice also that the Identical Three Crows pattern dropped to the number 5 position. Falling Three Methods, reflecting its name, dropped to the number 46 position with a ranking of -33%.

Using a prediction interval of seven days reversed the decline in successful patterns with 35 out of the 55, or 63%, ranked successful, as illustrated in Table 7-3. Notice also that the top two patterns were previously near the bottom in the previous tables.

Summary of the Three Stock Tables

What can be gleaned from the data in Tables 7-1, 7-2, and 7-3? Remember that the exact same data were used in each table and that only the prediction intervals were changed. As a result, we can make the following observations:

1. If a pattern rises and falls in the rankings when the prediction interval is changed, its usefulness is suspect for the data being used. For example, Downside Gap Three Methods moved from 39 when the prediction interval was at three days, to number 20 with the prediction interval at five, and then to 37 as the prediction interval increased to seven. Even though the jump up to 20 was not exceptional, it did show

that this pattern's predictive ability wasn't steady, which is what we are looking for in these tables.

2. Steady movement in a single direction in the rankings can be telling. Matching Low is a good example. In Table 7-1 it ranked at 44 with a negative 35.35% ranking score. As the prediction interval increased from three to five days, Matching Low moved up the rankings to 31. And at seven days, Matching Low was up to 24th place and a 8.71% ranking score. This says that the Matching Low reversal pattern tends to get better, relatively, with an increase in prediction interval. Said differently, Matching Low has staying power and tends to be longer term in its trend-reversal prediction capability.

    Meeting Lines+ is another good example of a pattern that moves up the list as the prediction interval is increased. Meeting Lines+ moved from 50 to 14, and then to the number 2 position. This indicates that Meeting Lines+ tends to be better at slightly longer term predictions of trend change. The only problem is that Meeting Lines+ occurred only twice, which makes the conclusion somewhat suspect.

    Identical Three Crows, while number 1 with the prediction interval at three, moved to number 5, and then down to number 50 when the prediction interval increased to seven days. This shows that it tends to be much better as a short term reversal indicator than as a longer term one.

3. Patterns that continue to remain in the same relative position are the most stable predictors of trend changes. Out of the first 15 patterns for a prediction interval of three days, 6 patterns remained in the top 15 for all three rankings. They were Three Black Crows, Three White Soldiers, Three Inside Up, Three Outside Down, Dark Cloud Cover, and Three Outside Up. These 6 reversal patterns consistently showed good performance over all prediction intervals tested.

At the other end of the spectrum, 6 patterns remained in the bottom 15 ranking for all three prediction intervals. They were Three Line Strike-, Doji Star+, Doji Star-, Three Stars in the South, Side-by-Side White Lines-, and Breakaway+. Three of these patterns, Three Stars in the South, Side-by-Side White Lines-, and Breakaway+, occurred only once in all of the data, so not much significance should be put on them.

It is also interesting to note that when the prediction interval was increased to nine days, only Three Black Crows, Three Inside Up, and Dark Cloud Cover remained in the top 15 ranking. Three Line Strike- and Side-by-Side White Lines- were the only patterns to remain in the bottom 15 ranking. The surprise came when the consistently poor performers, Three Stars in the South and Breakaway+, were in the number 1 and 3 positions, respectively.

Obviously, one could get overly analytical with the results. One should always strive to make observations that have at least a chance at being successful when additional data and/or intervals are used.

Candle Patterns and Futures

The candle pattern ranking for 41 different futures contracts was performed on over 49,000 days of data. Table 7-4 shows the results for a prediction interval of three days. Out of 62 possible candle patterns, 57 patterns were identified in this data. It is important to note that 7 patterns occurred only one or two times. Slightly more than half (32 out of 57) were deemed successful using the ranking system previously discussed. Here, just as with the stocks, two patterns had a 100% success rate. Kicking-, a reversal pattern, had only a single occurrence and should not be given much significance. Side-by-Side White Lines+, a continuation pattern, had a 100% success rate and a ranking score of 40.65%. Remember that continuation patterns have the trend working in their favor and therefore must perform exceptionally well to receive a high ranking score.

With the prediction interval at five days, 30 out of 57 patterns had positive ranking scores, as shown in Table 7-5. Note, however, that 4 patterns had 100% success. Because the number of occurrences of each of these patterns was small, their significance should be based upon how they performed over varying prediction intervals.

Table 7-4

CANDLE PATTERN RANKING

Interval: 3   41 Autoruns/C:\n2\csi\   Periods: 314

Rankings Based on Percent Improvement Over RANDOM Calls

No.	Type	Name	Total	Success	%Success	%Ranking
1	R-	Kicking-	1	1	100.00	246.02
2	R-	Three Black Crows-	12	9	75.00	159.52
3	R+	Morning Doji Star+	14	11	78.50	150.00
4	R+	Abandoned Baby+	4	3	75.00	138.85
5	R+	Three White Soldiers+	4	3	75.00	138.85
6	R+	Breakaway+	4	3	75.00	138.85
7	R-	Three Outside Down-	128	80	62.50	116.26
8	R+	Three Inside Up+	46	31	67.30	114.33
9	R+	Three Outside Up+	131	86	65.60	108.92
10	R-	Three Inside Down-	49	25	51.00	76.47
11	R-	Engulfing Pattern-	454	231	50.80	75.78
12	R+	Engulfing Pattern+	452	240	53.00	68.79
13	C	Side/Side White Lines+	4	4	100.00	40.65
14	R-	Dark Cloud Cover-	123	47	38.20	32.18
15	R+	Piercing Line+	111	46	41.40	31.85
16	R+	Belt Hold+	17	7	41.10	30.89
17	R+	Morning Star+	25	10	40.00	27.39
18	R-	Belt Hold-	22	8	36.30	25.61
19	C	Falling Three Methods-	17	14	82.30	19.97
20	R+	Harami Cross+	24	9	37.50	19.43
21	R-	Evening Star-	32	11	34.30	18.69
22	R-	Harami-	467	158	33.80	16.96
23	C	In Neck Line-	58	46	79.30	15.60
24	R-	Upside Gap Two Crows-	18	6	33.30	15.22
25	C	Separating Lines+	5	4	80.00	12.52
26	C	Upside Tasuki Gap+	88	66	75.00	5.49
27	C	On Neck Line-	43	31	72.00	4.96
28	R-	Evening Doji Star-	10	3	30.00	3.81
29	R+	Harami+	444	141	31.70	0.96
30	R-	Two Crows-	24	7	29.10	0.69
31	C	Rising Three Methods+	14	10	71.40	0.42
32	R+	Hammer+	175	55	31.40	0.00
33	C	UPside Gap 3 Methods+	10	7	70.00	-1.55
34	C	Separating Lines-	3	2	66.60	-2.92
35	C	Downside Tasuki Gap-	90	58	64.40	-6.12
36	R+	Inverted Hammer+	31	9	29.00	-7.64
37	R-	Hanging Man-	163	43	26.30	-9.00
38	R+	Doji Star+	21	6	28.50	-9.24
39	R-	Breakaway-	4	1	25.00	-13.49
40	C	DNside Gap 3 Methods-	22	13	59.00	-13.99
41	R-	Harami Cross-	30	7	23.30	-19.38
42	R+	Matching Low+	4	1	25.00	-20.38
43	C	Three Line Strike-	17	9	52.90	-22.89
44	C	Side/Side White Lines-	4	2	50.00	-27.11
45	R-	Shooting Star-	5	1	20.00	-30.80
46	R-	Deliberation-	20	3	15.00	-48.10
47	R-	Doji Star-	37	5	13.50	-53.29
48	C	Three Line Strike+	16	5	31.20	-56.12
49	R-	Meeting Lines-	8	1	12.50	-56.75
50	R+	Homing Pigeon+	24	2	8.30	-73.57
51	R+	Unique 3 River Bottom+	1	0	0.00	-100.00
52	R+	Meeting Lines+	3	0	0.00	-100.00
53	R+	Stick Sandwich+	2	0	0.00	-100.00
54	R-	Advance Block-	1	0	0.00	-100.00
55	R-	Abandoned Baby-	2	0	0.00	-100.00
56	R+	Concealing Swallow+	1	0	0.00	-100.00
57	R-	Identical 3 Crows-	1	0	0.00	-100.00

Table 7-5

CANDLE PATTERN RANKING
Interval: 5   41 Autoruns/C:\n2\csi\   Periods: 314

Rankings Based on Percent Improvement Over RANDOM Calls

No.	Type	Name	Total	Success	%Success	%Ranking
1	R-	Identical 3 Crows-	1	1	100.00	183.29
2	R-	Kicking-	1	1	100.00	183.29
3	R+	Breakaway+	4	4	100.00	161.10
4	R-	Breakaway-	4	3	75.00	112.46
5	R-	Three Black Crows-	12	8	66.60	88.67
6	R+	Morning Star+	25	17	68.00	77.55
7	R+	Morning Doji Star+	14	9	64.20	67.62
8	R-	Three Outside Down-	128	72	56.20	59.21
9	R-	Upside Gap Two Crows-	18	10	55.50	57.22
10	C	Side/Side White Lines+	4	4	100.00	54.56
11	R+	Three Outside Up+	131	76	58.00	51.44
12	R-	Engulfing Pattern-	453	238	52.50	48.73
13	R+	Three Inside Up+	46	26	56.50	47.52
14	R-	Abandoned Baby-	2	1	50.00	41.64
15	R-	Evening Star-	32	16	50.00	41.64
16	R+	Engulfing Pattern+	451	234	51.80	35.25
17	R+	Three White Soldiers+	4	2	50.00	30.55
18	R+	Abandoned Baby+	4	2	50.00	30.55
19	R-	Three Inside Down-	49	22	44.80	26.91
20	R+	Belt Hold+	17	8	47.00	22.72
21	C	Side/Side White Lines-	4	3	75.00	21.56
22	R-	Dark Cloud Cover-	122	49	40.10	13.60
23	R-	Shooting Star-	5	2	40.00	13.31
24	R+	Hammer+	174	74	42.50	10.97
25	R+	Inverted Hammer+	31	13	41.90	9.40
26	C	In Neck Line-	58	39	67.20	8.91
27	R+	Piercing Line+	111	46	41.40	8.09
28	R-	Harami-	467	177	37.90	7.37
29	R-	Two Crows-	24	9	37.50	6.23
30	R+	Harami+	442	178	40.20	4.96
31	C	Downside Tasuki Gap-	90	55	61.10	-0.97
32	C	Three Line Strike+	16	10	62.50	-3.40
33	C	Separating Lines+	5	3	60.00	-7.26
34	R-	Hanging Man-	163	53	32.50	-7.93
35	C	Upside Tasuki Gap+	88	52	59.00	-8.81
36	R+	Meeting Lines+	3	1	33.30	-13.05
37	R-	Evening Doji Star-	10	3	30.00	-15.01
38	R-	Doji Star-	37	11	29.70	-15.86
39	C	On Neck Line-	43	21	48.80	-20.91
40	C	UPside Gap 3 Methods+	10	5	50.00	-22.72
41	C	Three Line Strike-	17	8	47.00	-23.82
42	C	Falling Three Methods-	17	8	47.00	-23.82
43	R+	Doji Star+	21	6	28.50	-25.59
44	C	DNside Gap 3 Methods-	22	9	40.90	-33.71
45	R-	Harami Cross-	30	7	23.30	-33.99
46	R+	Matching Low+	4	1	25.00	-34.73
47	R+	Harami Cross+	24	6	25.00	-34.73
48	R-	Belt Hold-	22	5	22.70	-35.69
49	C	Rising Three Methods+	13	5	38.40	-40.65
50	R-	Deliberation-	20	3	15.00	-57.51
51	R-	Meeting Lines-	8	1	12.50	-64.59
52	R+	Homing Pigeon+	24	3	12.50	-67.36
53	R-	Advance Block-	1	0	0.00	-100.00
54	R+	Stick Sandwich+	2	0	0.00	-100.00
55	R+	Unique 3 River Bottom+	1	0	0.00	-100.00
56	C	Separating Lines-	3	0	0.00	-100.00
57	R+	Concealing Swallow+	1	0	0.00	-100.00

Table 7-6

```
                        CANDLE PATTERN RANKING
              Interval: 7     41 Autoruns/C:\n2\csi\    Periods: 314

        Rankings Based on Percent Improvement Over RANDOM Calls
```

No.	Type	Name	Total	Success	%Success	%Ranking
1	R-	Kicking-	1	1	100.00	155.75
2	R-	Advance Block-	1	1	100.00	155.75
3	R+	Concealing Swallow+	1	1	100.00	135.29
4	R-	Three Black Crows-	12	9	75.00	91.82
5	R+	Three White Soldiers+	4	3	75.00	76.47
6	R+	Breakaway+	4	3	75.00	76.47
7	C	Side/Side White Lines-	4	4	100.00	73.91
8	R+	Three Outside Up+	131	81	61.80	45.41
9	R-	Three Inside Down-	48	26	54.10	38.36
10	R+	Belt Hold+	17	10	58.80	38.35
11	R+	Three Inside Up+	46	27	58.60	37.88
12	R-	Evening Star-	32	17	53.10	35.81
13	R-	Engulfing Pattern-	453	235	51.80	32.48
14	R+	Morning Star+	25	14	56.00	31.76
15	R-	Three Outside Down-	128	66	51.50	31.71
16	C	UPside Gap 3 Methods+	10	8	80.00	31.36
17	R-	Meeting Lines-	8	4	50.00	27.88
18	R-	Abandoned Baby-	2	1	50.00	27.88
19	R-	Breakaway-	4	2	50.00	27.88
20	R+	Engulfing Pattern+	450	236	52.40	23.29
21	C	Side/Side White Lines+	4	3	75.00	23.15
22	C	In Neck Line-	57	39	68.40	18.96
23	R+	Inverted Hammer+	31	15	48.30	13.65
24	R-	Upside Gap Two Crows-	18	8	44.40	13.56
25	C	Three Line Strike+	16	11	68.70	12.81
26	R-	Harami-	465	199	42.70	9.21
27	R+	Hammer+	174	79	45.40	6.82
28	R-	Doji Star-	37	15	40.50	3.58
29	R-	Evening Doji Star-	10	4	40.00	2.30
30	R-	Harami Cross-	30	12	40.00	2.30
31	C	Falling Three Methods-	17	10	58.80	2.26
32	C	On Neck Line-	43	25	58.10	1.04
33	C	Rising Three Methods+	13	8	61.50	0.99
34	R+	Morning Doji Star+	14	6	42.80	0.71
35	C	Upside Tasuki Gap+	88	54	61.30	0.66
36	R-	Dark Cloud Cover-	122	48	39.30	0.51
37	R-	Hanging Man-	163	64	39.20	0.26
38	R+	Harami+	441	188	42.60	0.24
39	C	Downside Tasuki Gap-	89	51	57.30	-0.35
40	C	Separating Lines+	5	3	60.00	-1.48
41	C	Three Line Strike-	17	9	52.90	-8.00
42	R+	Harami Cross+	24	9	37.50	-11.76
43	R+	Piercing Line+	111	41	36.90	-13.18
44	R-	Belt Hold-	22	7	31.80	-18.67
45	C	DNside Gap 3 Methods-	22	10	45.40	-21.04
46	R+	Meeting Lines+	3	1	33.30	-21.65
47	R-	Deliberation-	20	6	30.00	-23.27
48	R-	Two Crows-	24	7	29.10	-25.58
49	R+	Doji Star+	21	6	28.50	-32.94
50	R+	Homing Pigeon+	24	6	25.00	-41.18
51	R+	Abandoned Baby+	4	1	25.00	-41.18
52	R+	Matching Low+	4	1	25.00	-41.18
53	R-	Shooting Star-	5	1	20.00	-48.85
54	R+	Stick Sandwich+	2	0	0.00	-100.00
55	R+	Unique 3 River Bottom+	1	0	0.00	-100.00
56	C	Separating Lines-	3	0	0.00	-100.00
57	R-	Identical 3 Crows-	1	0	0.00	-100.00

Setting the prediction interval at seven days gave 38 successful patterns, or over 66%. Again, 4 patterns had successes of 100%, but also notice that it wasn't the same 4 patterns as in Table 7-5.

Summary of the Three Futures Tables

1. As when analyzing stocks, patterns that jump around in the rankings should be noted. Shooting Star started out with a rank of 45 when the prediction interval was three days. When the prediction interval was moved up to five days, Shooting Star improved to a ranking of 23. Finally, with the prediction interval at seven days, Shooting Star dropped to a low of 53. This type of volatility shows that the Shooting Star should not be relied upon when used with this data.

2. Steady movement, whether up the list or down, will help identify patterns that may be used for shorter or longer predictions. The first pattern to demonstrate this trait is Morning Doji Star. It starts out with a ranking of 3, then moves down slightly to a ranking of 7, and finally drops to a ranking of 34. This says that Morning Doji Star is best when used for short prediction intervals.

    In contrast, Side-by-Side White Lines- starts out with a ranking of 44, moves up to a ranking of 21, and then continues up to a ranking of 7. These significant moves strongly suggest that Side-by-Side White Lines- is best at making longer term predictions. As you may remember from Chapter 4, Side-by-Side White Lines- would normally show a somewhat bullish pattern in that there are two normally bullish white lines in a row. This probably accounts for its longer term perspective on the trend. Even though it appears as a bullish set of days, it is correctly calling the downtrend to continue.

3. Patterns that were stable in their rankings are the best overall performers. Only 7 of the top 15 patterns when the prediction interval was three days remained that high for all three tests. They were Kicking-, Three Black Crows, Breakaway+, Three Outside Up, Three Inside Up, Engulfing Pattern-, and Three Outside Down. Of these 7 patterns,

Kicking- had only a single occurrence and Breakaway+ showed up only four times.

Of the patterns in the bottom 15 for the prediction interval of three, only 4 remained throughout. They were Deliberation, Homing Pigeon, Stick Sandwich, and Unique Three River Bottom. Of these 4 patterns, only Deliberation and Homing Pigeon had a significant number of occurrences.

When the prediction interval was increased to nine days, only 4 patterns remained in the top 15: Kicking-, Breakaway+, Three Black Crows, and Three Outside Up. In the bottom 15 ranking, only two showed up: Homing Pigeon and Unique Three River Bottom.

Individual Stock Analysis

The next chapter shows the actual trading results on numerous stocks when candle patterns and indicators were used for the trading signals. From the 100 stocks shown in Table 8.1, the stock with the best trading gains based solely on candle patterns was picked for the following example. If you look down the first column labeled %AvGn-CS, you will see the average percentage gain per trade for each stock. The best average gain per trade was TDY (Teledyne). Therefore, the candle pattern statistics for over three years of daily data on TDY for the three prediction intervals of three, five, and seven days are shown in Tables 7-7, 7-8, and 7-9.

With individual stocks or futures, patterns that maintain a positive ranking throughout the prediction intervals can be looked upon as good patterns for that particular stock or commodity. The Engulfing Pattern+, while slowly moving down the ranking list as prediction intervals increased, maintained fairly good readings throughout. The Hanging Man also tended to maintain its success. The Hammer was not great, but it was consistent with each prediction interval. The other patterns did not appear often enough to provide meaningful information.

Table 7-7

CANDLE PATTERN RANKING
Interval: 3   1 Autoruns/C:\n2\sp100\   Periods: 821

Rankings Based on Percent Improvement Over RANDOM Calls

No.	Type	Name	Total	Success	%Success	%Ranking
1	R+	Engulfing Pattern+	12	7	58.30	86.86
2	R+	Belt Hold+	6	3	50.00	60.26
3	R+	Harami Cross+	2	1	50.00	60.26
4	R-	Belt Hold-	4	2	50.00	53.37
5	C	Three Line Strike+	1	1	100.00	48.37
6	C	UPside Gap 3 Methods+	1	1	100.00	48.37
7	C	On Neck Line-	1	1	100.00	45.35
8	R+	Hammer+	12	5	41.60	33.33
9	R-	Hanging Man-	15	5	33.30	2.15
10	R-	Harami Cross-	3	1	33.30	2.15
11	R-	Harami-	19	5	26.30	-19.33
12	C	Rising Three Methods+	2	1	50.00	-25.82
13	C	In Neck Line-	2	1	50.00	-27.33
14	R-	Engulfing Pattern-	9	2	22.20	-31.90
15	R-	Evening Star-	1	0	0.00	-100.00
16	R+	Harami+	1	0	0.00	-100.00
17	R+	Doji Star+	1	0	0.00	-100.00
18	R-	Doji Star-	1	0	0.00	-100.00
19	R-	Three Outside Down-	2	0	0.00	-100.00
20	R+	Inverted Hammer+	1	0	0.00	-100.00

Table 7-8

CANDLE PATTERN RANKING
Interval: 5   1 Autoruns/C:\n2\sp100\   Periods: 821

Rankings Based on Percent Improvement Over RANDOM Calls

No.	Type	Name	Total	Success	%Success	%Ranking
1	R+	Harami Cross+	2	2	100.00	172.48
2	R-	Harami Cross-	3	2	66.60	72.54
3	C	Three Line Strike+	1	1	100.00	62.87
4	C	On Neck Line-	1	1	100.00	57.98
5	R+	Engulfing Pattern+	12	6	50.00	36.24
6	R-	Belt Hold-	4	2	50.00	29.53
7	R-	Harami-	19	9	47.30	22.54
8	R-	Hanging Man-	15	7	46.60	20.73
9	R-	Engulfing Pattern-	9	4	44.40	15.03
10	R+	Hammer+	12	4	33.30	-9.26
11	C	Rising Three Methods+	2	1	50.00	-18.57
12	C	In Neck Line-	2	1	50.00	-21.01
13	R+	Belt Hold+	6	1	16.60	-54.77
14	R-	Evening Star-	1	0	0.00	-100.00
15	R+	Harami+	1	0	0.00	-100.00
16	R+	Doji Star+	1	0	0.00	-100.00
17	R-	Doji Star-	1	0	0.00	-100.00
18	R-	Three Outside Down-	2	0	0.00	-100.00
19	R+	Inverted Hammer+	1	0	0.00	-100.00
20	C	UPside Gap 3 Methods+	1	0	0.00	-100.00

Table 7-9

```
                          CANDLE PATTERN RANKING
                Interval: 7      1 Autoruns/C:\n2\sp100\      Periods: 821

            Rankings Based on Percent Improvement Over RANDOM Calls
```

No.	Type	Name	Total	Success	%Success	%Ranking
1	R+	Harami Cross+	2	2	100.00	139.23
2	R-	Evening Star-	1	1	100.00	126.76
3	C	Three Line Strike+	1	1	100.00	78.89
4	C	UPside Gap 3 Methods+	1	1	100.00	78.89
5	C	Rising Three Methods+	2	2	100.00	78.89
6	C	On Neck Line-	1	1	100.00	71.82
7	R-	Harami Cross-	3	2	66.60	51.02
8	R+	Engulfing Pattern+	12	7	58.30	39.47
9	R-	Hanging Man-	15	8	53.30	20.86
10	R+	Belt Hold+	6	3	50.00	19.62
11	R-	Harami-	19	10	52.60	19.27
12	R-	Three Outside Down-	2	1	50.00	13.38
13	R+	Hammer+	12	5	41.60	-0.48
14	C	In Neck Line-	2	1	50.00	-14.09
15	R-	Belt Hold-	4	1	25.00	-43.31
16	R-	Engulfing Pattern-	9	2	22.20	-49.66
17	R+	Doji Star+	1	0	0.00	-100.00
18	R+	Harami+	1	0	0.00	-100.00
19	R-	Doji Star-	1	0	0.00	-100.00
20	R+	Inverted Hammer+	1	0	0.00	-100.00

8 | Candlestick Filtering

Candlestick filtering offers a method of trading with candlesticks that is supported by other popular technical tools for analysis. Filtering is a concept that has been used in many other forms of technical analysis and is now a proven method with candlesticks.

If there is any fault with using a single method for market timing and analysis, it most certainly will also be a fault with candlesticks. Just like any price-based technical indicator based upon a singular concept, candlesticks will not work all of the time. When indicators are combined or used in conjunction with one another, the results can only improve. Again, candlesticks are no different: when used with another indicator, the results are superb.

The Filtering Concept

The filtering concept was developed to assist the analyst in removing premature candle patterns, or for that matter, eliminate most of the early patterns. Because candle patterns are intensely dependent upon the underlying trend of the market, lengthy trends in price will usually cause early

241

pattern signals, just like most technical indicators. Something else had to be used to assist in the qualification of the candle pattern signals. Most technical analysts use more that one indicator to confirm their signals, so why not do the same with candle patterns? The answer is the use of technical indicators. While appearing obvious, technical indicators did not provide the "how" answer to the problem, only the "what."

The following discussion will try to explain the answer to the "how" question. Most indicators have a buy and sell definition to help in their interpretation and use. There is a point prior to a buy or sell signal that is normally a better place for a signal to fire, but it is difficult to define. Most, if not all, indicators lag the market somewhat. This is because the components of indicator construction are the underlying data itself. If an indicator's parameters are set too tight, the result will be too many bad signals, or whipsaws. Therefore, a pre-signal area was calculated based upon thresholds and/or indicator values, whether positive or negative.

Once an indicator reaches its defined pre-signal area, it has been primed to await its firing signal. The amount of time an indicator will be in the pre-signal area cannot be determined. The only certainty is that once an indicator reaches its pre-signal area, it will eventually produce a trading signal (buy or sell). Statistically, it has been found that the longer an indicator is in its pre-signal area, the better the actual buy or sell signal will be.

The pre-signal area is the filtering area for each individual indicator; its fingerprint. Each indicator has a different fingerprint. If the indicator is in the buying pre-signal area, only bullish candle patterns will be filtered. Likewise, if an indicator is in the selling pre-signal area, only bearish candle patterns are filtered.

Figure 8-1

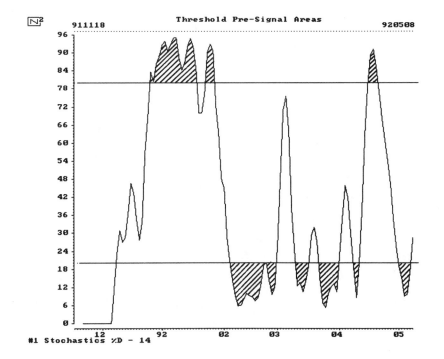

Pre-Signal Areas

For threshold-based indicators, the pre-signal area is the area between the indicator and the thresholds, both above and below (Figure 8-1).

For oscillators, the pre-signal area is defined as the area after the indicator crosses the zero line until it crosses the moving average or smoothing used to define the trading signals (Figure 8-2).

Figure 8-2

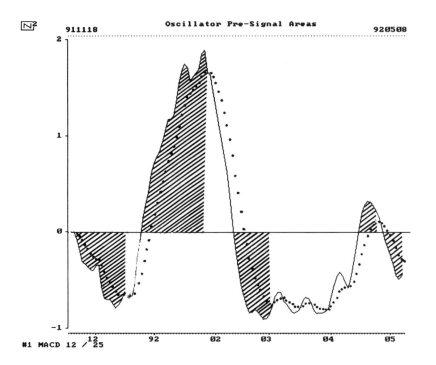

Indicators

The indicators used to filter candle patterns should be easily available and simple to define. They must perform in a manner that enables one to determine areas of buying and areas of selling. These are often referred to as overbought and oversold areas. Indicators such as Welles Wilder's RSI (Relative Strength Index) and George Lane's %K and %D (stochastics) are exceptionally good for candlestick filtering because they both remain between 0 and 100. At the end of this chapter, many other indicators will be shown to demonstrate the filtering concept. Because RSI and stochastics are so widely known and used, more detail will be provided on their construction and use in filtering.

Wilder's RSI

J. Welles Wilder developed the Relative Strength Index (RSI) in the late 1970s. It has been a popular indicator, with many different interpretations. It is a simple measurement that expresses the relative strength of the current price movement as increasing from 0 to 100. Basically, it averages the up days and the down days. Up and down days are determined by the day's close relative to the previous day's close.

Wilder favored the use of the 14-period measurement because it represents one-half of a natural cycle in the market. He also set the significant levels of the indicator at 30 and 70. The lower level indicates an imminent upturn and the upper level, a downturn.

A plot of RSI can be interpreted using many of the classic bar chart formations, such as head and shoulders. Divergence with price within the

Figure 8-3

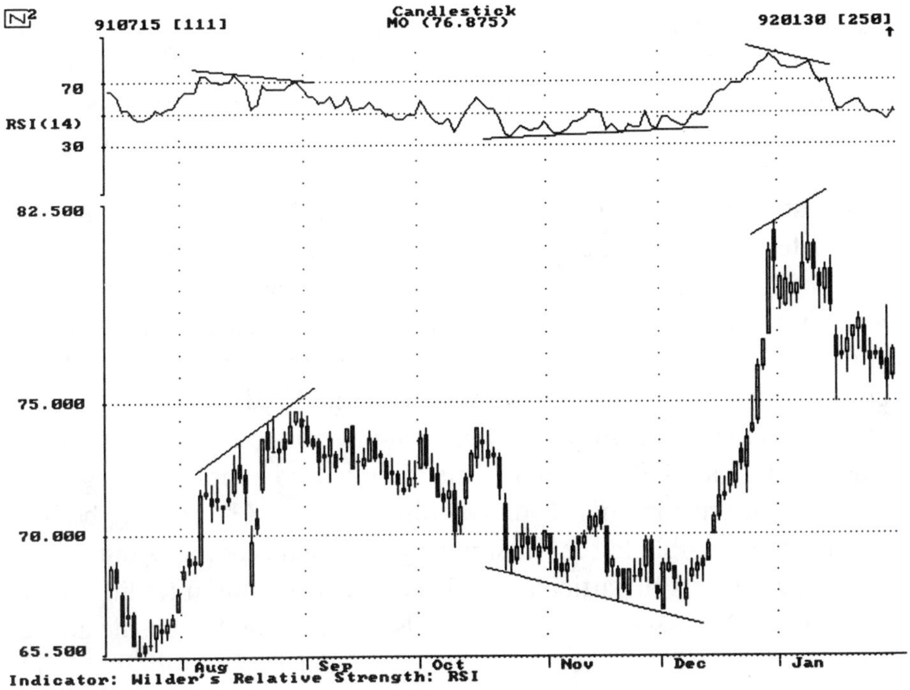

Indicator: Wilder's Relative Strength: RSI

period used to calculate the RSI works well, if the divergence takes place near the upper or lower regions of the indicator.

Many stock-charting services show RSI calculations based on 14 periods. Some commodity chart services prefer to use 9 periods. If you can determine the dominant cycle of the data, that value would be a good period to use for RSI. The levels (thresholds) for determining market turning points can also be moved. Using levels of 35 and 65 seem to work better for stocks, whereas the original levels of 30 and 70 are better for futures.

In the chart of Philip Morris (MO), presented in Figure 8-3, the divergence of the 14-day RSI with the general price trends is quite obvious. Whenever the RSI gets into or near the thresholds, a change in the trend of prices is soon to follow.

Lane's Stochastic Oscillator: %D

George Lane developed stochastics many years ago. A stochastic, in this sense, is an oscillator that measures the relative position of the closing price within the daily range. In simple terms, where is the close relative to the range of prices over the last x periods? Just like RSI, 14 periods seems to be a popular choice.

Stochastics is based on the commonly accepted observation that closing prices tend to cluster near the day's high prices as an upwards move gains strength and near the day's lows during a decline. For instance, when a market is about to turn from up to down, highs are often higher, but the closing price settles near the low. This makes the stochastic oscillator different from most oscillators, which are normalized representations of the relative strength, the difference between the close and a selected trend.

The calculation of %D is simply the three period simple moving average of %K. It is customarily displayed directly over %K, making both of them almost impossible to see. Interpreting stochastics requires familiarity with the way it reacts in particular markets. The usual initial trading signal occurs when %D crosses the extreme bands (75 to 85 on the upside and 15 to 25 on the downside). The actual trading signal is not made until %K

Figure 8-4

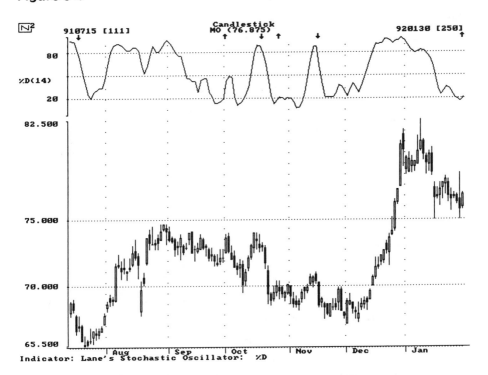

crosses %D. Even though the extreme zones help assure an adverse reaction of minimum size, the crossing of the two lines acts in a way similar to dual moving averages.

In Figure 8-4, the same chart of Philip Morris (MO) used in the RSI example, we can see how good Lane's %D is at oscillating with the prices to areas of overbought and oversold.

Filtering Parameters

Many powerful trading and back-testing software packages are available today. Some optimize indicators by curve-fitting the data, while others utilize money-management techniques. A few have advanced methods that concentrate on all possibilities. It is not going to be the purpose here to

247

amplify the faults or hail the innovations of this type of analysis. The method used will be simple and straightforward in concept.

Three trading systems will be utilized in these tests: candle patterns, indicators, and filtered candlesticks. Each will use the same methodology of buying, selling, selling short, and then covering so that a system is in the market at all times. While this is not always a good way to trade, it is used here to show how filtered candlesticks will usually outperform the other two systems. Also, the trading results are shown as if there were a closing trade on the last day of the data to give you a feel for the complete trading history.

Additionally, a signal is generated whenever the appropriate reference indicator reaches the prescribed parameters. That is, the indicator must have gone above (or below) the threshold and then cross it again in the opposite direction. For example, when %D goes above 80, it has entered the pre-signal area and the sell filter is turned on for the candle patterns. Any candle pattern that gives a sell signal when %D is above 80 will be registered as a filtered signal. Similarly, whenever %D goes below 20, it has entered the pre-signal area and the buy filter is turned on. Any bullish candle patterns that appear will be considered filtered patterns. The thresholds of 20 and 80 were used here only for purposes of explanation.

Each of the indicators requires a setting for the number of days (periods) to be used in their calculation. As mentioned earlier, this value should reflect the basic cycle of the market being analyzed. Two additional values need to be set: the upper and lower thresholds just mentioned. These are the settings that determine the values that the indicator must reach or exceed before it will filter a candle pattern.

Initially, commonly accepted values will be used: a 14-day %D, first with thresholds of 20 and 80 and then with thresholds of 65 and 35 on different data. The data used will be the stocks of the S&P 100 Index and the 30 stocks of the Dow Industrial Average. The S&P 100 database started at the beginning of 1989 and ended on March 31, 1992. The Dow Industrials database began on April 24, 1990, and ended on March 31, 1992.

Filtering Examples

From Table 8-1 you can see that trading each stock using candle patterns for the advice resulted in 67 stocks with positive percentage gains and 33 losers. These numbers came simply from counting the positive and negative results in the first column. Trading strictly on the candle pattern signals resulted in an average of 37.1 trades, with an average gain per trade of 0.40%.

Trading the same 100 stocks using only %D for the trading signals resulted in only 53 stocks that were winners and 47 losers. The number of average trades was reduced to 30.1, with an average gain of 0.02% per trade.

Using the filtering concept for the trading signals resulted in 62 winners and 38 losers. This was not as good as using the candle patterns by themselves, but was much better than using signals generated strictly from the stochastic indicator %D. The average number of trades was 13.7, which is better than candle patterns or %D by over 50%. The average gain per trade was 0.60% which, again, is significantly better than the average gain from the other two trading methods.

What does all of this really tell you? First, by filtering the candle patterns with an indicator, such as %D, the number of trades is significantly reduced. Compared to candle patterns alone, the reduction was over 63%, and compared to trades using the indicator %D alone, the reduction was over 54%. Second, filtering increased the average gain per trade. The increase over candle patterns alone was 50% and the increase over the %D was over 30 times as great.

You should not ignore or forget what is known about using statistics to make a point; they can be manipulated to show whatever results the author is trying to make. We all know that an average gain of 0.6% would quickly disappear when we included commissions, slippage, and the like. The simplicity of these calculations, though, shows one very important point: It is the relationship of the numbers with each other that is important, not the actual numbers. This relationship, taken as an average of the values derived from 100 different stocks, is the proof needed to support the filtering concept.

Table 8-1

Filtering Statistics

100 Tickers   1340   Periods Indicator: %D(14)   Buy Line: 20 Sell LIne: 80

Ticker	%Gain/CS	%AvGn-CS	%Gain/Ind	%AvGn-Ind	%Gain/Fil	%AvGn-Fil
AA	47.690/40	= 1.1923	82.100/38	= 2.1605	89.040/19	= 4.6863
AEP	19.840/34	= 0.5835	-35.800/34	=-1.0529	8.9700/14	= 0.6407
AGC	-9.690/40	=-0.2423	9.7800/30	= 0.3260	8.0500/17	= 0.4735
AIG	6.8700/41	= 0.1676	12.320/30	= 0.4107	-59.940/14	=-4.2814
AIT	9.3800/33	= 0.2842	42.320/27	= 1.5674	21.980/10	= 2.1980
AMP	-34.440/48	=-0.7175	27.650/33	= 0.8379	19.660/15	= 1.3107
AN	47.330/38	= 1.2455	-32.510/35	=-0.9289	10.760/7	= 1.5371
ARC	48.740/42	= 1.1605	57.680/36	= 1.6022	4.0900/12	= 0.3408
AVP	-105.26/35	=-3.0074	92.000/34	= 2.7059	-17.930/12	=-1.4942
AXP	81.570/43	= 1.8970	38.510/29	= 1.3279	113.36/16	= 7.0850
BA	-16.960/29	=-0.5848	26.750/31	= 0.8629	108.53/20	= 5.4265
BAC	-21.860/33	=-0.6624	-82.550/21	=-3.9310	-44.550/11	=-4.0500
BAX	44.410/43	= 1.0328	-23.130/27	=-0.8567	52.120/15	= 3.4747
BC	24.620/39	= 0.6313	-14.760/30	=-0.4920	190.74/18	= 10.597
BCC	83.770/46	= 1.8211	40.060/26	= 1.5408	25.070/14	= 1.7907
BDK	-77.760/44	=-1.7673	131.07/36	= 3.6408	-31.490/16	=-1.9681
BEL	52.780/48	= 1.0996	-22.200/28	=-0.7929	29.140/16	= 1.8213
BHI	114.57/38	= 3.0150	9.1300/36	= 0.2536	30.540/14	= 2.1814
BMY	41.450/36	= 1.1514	54.950/33	= 1.6652	-31.740/5	= -6.3480
BNI	9.0000/36	= 0.2500	-44.460/27	=-1.6467	-49.100/9	= -5.4556
BS	58.150/45	= 1.2922	-58.090/32	=-1.8153	-8.7100/12	=-0.7258
CCB	18.560/35	= 0.5303	3.8700/29	= 0.1334	-35.480/14	=-2.5343
CCI	39.360/40	= 0.9840	-40.970/38	=-1.0782	42.240/21	= 2.0114
CDA	38.770/37	= 1.0478	233.73/33	= 7.0827	67.140/14	= 4.7957
CGP	53.650/48	= 1.1177	55.500/36	= 1.5417	43.730/19	= 2.3016
CHA	54.160/41	= 1.3210	65.230/28	= 2.3296	70.600/19	= 3.7158
CI	16.320/44	= 0.3709	13.080/28	= 0.4671	-4.3100/16	=-0.2694
CL	20.010/51	= 0.3924	-49.560/25	=-1.9824	-8.2400/19	=-0.4337
CSC	-42.050/43	=-0.9779	12.360/33	= 0.3745	38.810/19	= 2.0426
CWE	-10.930/33	=-0.3312	-68.300/23	=-2.9696	11.540/12	= 0.9617
DAL	-15.960/42	=-0.3800	86.830/36	= 2.4119	-2.3100/14	=-0.1650
DD	-25.940/45	=-0.5764	-46.350/29	=-1.5983	14.070/12	= 1.1725
DEC	30.880/37	= 0.8346	41.410/29	= 1.4279	75.850/14	= 5.4179
DIS	-36.790/28	=-1.3139	-55.110/21	=-2.6243	-45.950/13	=-3.5346
DOW	-146.10/29	=-5.0379	-15.670/32	=-0.4897	-16.120/9	= -1.7911
EK	-3.4000/30	=-0.1133	26.600/31	= 0.8581	32.730/10	= 3.2730
ETR	-12.940/32	=-0.4044	-25.660/25	=-1.0264	-62.480/6	= -10.413
F	-58.800/32	=-1.8375	16.150/28	= 0.5768	-85.530/9	= -9.503
FDX	29.690/40	= 0.7423	64.750/32	= 2.0234	-4.0700/15	=-0.2713
FLR	44.220/36	= 1.2283	45.310/35	= 1.2946	132.12/18	= 7.3400
FNB	91.740/41	= 2.2376	23.440/27	= 0.8681	84.600/21	= 4.0286
GD	67.350/39	= 1.7269	-23.430/25	=-0.9372	-32.300/14	=-2.3071
GE	8.8000/23	= 0.3826	-14.610/29	=-0.5038	-43/7	= -6.1429
GM	-25.110/27	=-0.9300	21.580/31	= 0.6961	24.930/11	= 2.2664
GWF	83.550/44	= 1.8989	-80.230/30	=-2.6743	-107.71/12	=-8.9758
HAL	39.060/38	= 1.0279	88.670/32	= 2.7709	16.060/14	= 1.1471
HM	-9.810/38	=-0.2582	-35.270/32	=-1.1022	97.200/17	= 5.7176
HNZ	-27.660/42	=-0.6586	-29.680/23	=-1.2904	11.810/16	= 0.7381
HON	-21.150/31	=-0.6823	-3.5600/28	=-0.1271	-10.480/10	=-1.0480
HRS	41.300/41	= 1.0073	61.480/31	= 1.9832	9.1300/14	= 0.6521
HUM	62.090/39	= 1.5921	48.970/31	= 1.5797	161.86/20	= 8.0930
HWP	-18/22	=-0.8182	-106.32/26	=-4.0892	9.2400/10	= 0.9240
I	-74.760/38	=-1.9674	-35.580/28	=-1.2707	-45.430/20	=-2.2715
IBM	11.380/31	= 0.3671	12.030/31	= 0.3881	14.910/11	= 1.3555
IFF	-25.540/43	=-0.5940	32.710/33	= 0.9912	4/15	= 0.2667
IMA	19.640/33	= 0.5952	-23.540/28	=-0.8407	-14.590/13	=-1.1223
IP	46.850/31	= 1.5113	34.280/26	= 1.3185	35.360/13	= 2.7200
ITT	74.590/33	= 2.2603	25.560/36	= 0.7100	49.630/15	= 3.3087
JNJ	16.830/35	= 0.4809	-37.890/28	=-1.3532	-13.870/13	=-1.0669

Table 8-1 (continued)

Ticker	%Gain/CS	%AvGn-CS	%Gain/Ind	%AvGn-Ind	%Gain/Fil	%AvGn-Fil
KM	69.950/41 = 1.7061		31.310/31 = 1.0100		-16.390/16 =-1.0244	
KO	-34.090/34 =-1.0026		-61.820/24 =-2.5758		-102.14/11 = -9.285	
LIT	64.830/39 = 1.6623		40.910/42 = 0.9740		56.080/18 = 3.1156	
LTD	131.97/40 = 3.2993		-93.690/25 =-3.7476		-6.4000/16 =-0.4000	
MCD	35.690/40 = 0.8922		-33.790/30 =-1.1263		-7.3300/17 =-0.4312	
MCIC	147.67/37 = 3.9911		-10.350/32 =-0.3234		142.83/17 = 8.4018	
MER	65.940/36 = 1.8317		26.110/28 = 0.9325		37.920/20 = 1.8960	
MMM	46.860/35 = 1.3389		15.470/31 = 0.4990		51.840/13 = 3.9877	
MOB	43.720/47 = 0.9302		60.820/35 = 1.7377		25.260/17 = 1.4859	
MRK	-42.780/31 =-1.3800		-44.460/22 =-2.0209		-26.960/7 = -3.8514	
MTC	-25.090/27 =-0.9293		-24.230/25 =-0.9692		-49.560/9 = -5.5067	
NSC	35.660/31 = 1.1503		16.720/30 = 0.5573		58.970/17 = 3.4688	
NSM	-166.31/29 =-5.7348		-54.080/22 =-2.4582		-69.310/6 = -11.552	
NT	-37.080/37 =-1.0022		52.680/35 = 1.5051		42.920/13 = 3.3015	
OXY	-5.2100/34 =-0.1532		-95.790/22 =-4.3541		35.700/12 = 2.9750	
PCI	59.350/27 = 2.1981		-39.070/30 =-1.3023		10.510/11 = 0.9555	
PEP	48.670/40 = 1.2168		-64.410/29 =-2.2210		-8.0600/19 =-0.4242	
PRD	94.990/43 = 2.2091		35.510/32 = 1.1097		6.8300/11 = 0.6209	
PRI	88.500/31 = 2.8548		61.500/17 = 3.6176		-18.870/10 =-1.8870	
RAL	20.980/42 = 0.4995		-14.600/33 =-0.4424		41.410/17 = 2.4359	
ROK	67.470/43 = 1.5691		-54.640/36 =-1.5178		47.540/12 = 3.9617	
RTN	20.710/41 = 0.5051		-17.510/30 =-0.5837		36.190/15 = 2.4127	
S	-9.540/39 =-0.2446		-65.700/24 =-2.7375		-26.360/13 =-2.0277	
SKY	8.6600/38 = 0.2279		65.150/36 = 1.8097		-5.6200/17 =-0.3306	
SLB	-11.320/33 =-0.3430		126.96/39 = 3.2554		39.730/9 = 4.4144	
SO	-3.4300/35 =-0.0980		2.8500/25 = 0.1140		0.9200/12 = 0.0767	
T	-78/23 =-3.3913		58.960/29 = 2.0331		-32.240/9 = -3.5822	
TAN	31.440/34 = 0.9247		170.86/41 = 4.1673		72.490/19 = 3.8153	
TDY	147.34/36 = 4.0928		151.03/30 = 5.0343		112.80/7 = 16.114	
TEK	-18.000/35 =-0.5143		-29.300/26 =-1.1269		15.590/15 = 1.0393	
TOY	5.4200/33 = 0.1642		-45.240/35 =-1.2926		35.420/9 = 3.9356	
TXN	115.95/35 = 3.3129		-26.990/29 =-0.9307		118.08/17 = 6.9459	
UAL	60.960/32 = 1.9050		71.950/36 = 1.9986		-84.110/14 =-6.0079	
UIS	-30.310/30 =-1.0103		-253.25/22 =-11.511		-71.730/14 =-5.1236	
UPJ	29.830/38 = 0.7850		-36.960/26 =-1.4215		14.430/10 = 1.4430	
UTX	63.830/35 = 1.8237		92.380/37 = 2.4968		50.080/13 = 3.8523	
WMB	-0.8200/52 =-0.0158		41.210/36 = 1.1447		73.800/17 = 4.3412	
WMT	12.000/34 = 0.3529		-78.470/28 =-2.8025		-24.860/8 = -3.1075	
WY	4.5100/43 = 0.1049		-25.080/28 =-0.8957		-58.990/11 =-5.3627	
XON	-8.5400/40 =-0.2135		-35.710/27 =-1.3226		27.000/10 = 2.7000	
XRX	-73.810/32 =-2.3066		63.880/33 = 1.9358		8.9600/17 = 0.5271	

```
Trades/Gains:    37.1/  0.40         30.1/  0.02         13.7/  0.60
(Averages)

Tickers - C:\n2\sp100\      890103 TO 920331      Report: 04-05-1992 @ 17:50:54
```

Table 8-1 showed the results of the filtering concept by averaging the data on the 100 stocks of the S&P 100 Index. To keep the number of tables and the amount of information to a reasonable number, the next example will use the 30 stocks that make up the Dow Industrials.

Trading results for the 30 blue chip stocks that make up the Dow Industrial Average are shown in Table 8-2. The threshold values were changed slightly to open the signal area for the filtering to take place. Results similar to those using the S&P 100 stocks appear using just these 30 stocks. Trading strictly using candle patterns for buy and sell signals resulted in an average of 21.1 trades over the two-year period, with an average per-trade gain of 0.02%. Using the indicator %D gave an average number of trades of 23.7, with an average gain (loss) per trade of negative 0.46%. Finally, using the filtered candle patterns as the trading device

Table 8-2   Filtering Statistics

30 Tickers   1340   Periods Indicator: %D(14)   Buy Line: 30 Sell LIne: 70

Ticker	%Gain/CS	%AvGn-CS	%Gain/Ind	%AvGn-Ind	%Gain/Fil	%AvGn-Fil
AA	30.880/27 = 1.1437		62.420/26 = 2.4008		29.450/16 = 1.8406	
ALD	-29.060/21 =-1.3838		-11.820/27 =-0.4378		-45.670/10 =-4.5670	
AXP	86.480/27 = 3.2030		-53.460/21 =-2.5457		62.140/13 = 4.7800	
BA	-30.040/15 =-2.0027		-33.640/28 =-1.2014		1.1800/10 = 0.1180	
BS	55.940/25 = 2.2376		1.4100/25 = 0.0564		-33.110/9 = -3.6789	
CAT	-36.410/19 =-1.9163		5.0700/24 = 0.2113		-26.550/8 = -3.3188	
CHV	6.8900/29 = 0.2376		-2.2900/24 =-0.0954		25.320/16 = 1.5825	
DD	-20.660/27 =-0.7652		-51/17 = -3		-2.1900/15 =-0.1460	
DIS	-20.810/13 =-1.6008		-33.760/20 =-1.6880		-12.650/10 =-1.2650	
EK	-21.500/15 =-1.4333		22.630/27 = 0.8381		-11.380/9 = -1.2644	
GE	9.3900/12 = 0.7825		23.900/26 = 0.9192		-8.8700/5 = -1.7740	
GM	3.2600/18 = 0.1811		-8.4400/25 =-0.3376		50.980/11 = 4.6345	
GT	-42.200/19 =-2.2211		-40.190/22 =-1.8268		-15.560/11 =-1.4145	
IBM	2.9300/22 = 0.1332		33.430/21 = 1.5919		19.250/10 = 1.9250	
IP	39.790/18 = 2.2106		-18.600/19 =-0.9789		49.110/13 = 3.7777	
JPM	36.270/24 = 1.5113		-23.820/21 =-1.1343		51.770/10 = 5.1770	
KO	-4.2100/21 =-0.2005		-45.480/22 =-2.0673		-35.450/7 = -5.0643	
MCD	16.580/25 = 0.6632		-2.8300/21 =-0.1348		-0.2900/15 =-0.0193	
MMM	35.220/25 = 1.4088		-25.220/24 =-1.0508		10.860/10 = 1.0860	
MO	9.2600/20 = 0.4630		-27.940/21 =-1.3305		-25.820/5 = -5.1640	
MRK	-52.900/16 =-3.3063		-22.080/19 =-1.1621		-30.250/8 = -3.7813	
PG	-14.220/15 =-0.9480		-15.740/29 =-0.5428		-49/7 = -7	
S	-10.910/26 =-0.4196		-62.430/18 =-3.4683		-7.8700/12 =-0.6558	
T	-40.380/12 =-3.3650		-50.950/23 =-2.2152		10.050/7 = 1.4357	
TX	10.840/21 = 0.5162		-9.600/27 =-0.3556		20.510/14 = 1.4650	
UK	-25.700/27 =-0.9519		95.040/29 = 3.2772		30.390/10 = 3.0390	
UTX	58.920/21 = 2.8057		13.280/27 = 0.4919		43.640/12 = 3.6367	
WX	89.440/27 = 3.3126		61.730/32 = 1.9291		57.200/14 = 4.0857	
XON	-18.250/24 =-0.7604		-39.700/22 =-1.8045		7.8100/10 = 0.7810	
Z	20.390/21 = 0.9710		42.430/23 = 1.8448		71.520/11 = 6.5018	

Trades/Gains: 21.1/   0.02   23.7/ -0.46   10.6/   0.23
(Averages)

Tickers - C:\n2\dow\   900424 TO 920331   Report: 04-06-1992 @ 06:44:09

yielded an average number of trades of only 10.6, with an average gain per trade of 0.23%. Again, it must be stressed that it is the relationship of these numbers that is important, not their actual values.

Individual Stock Analysis

Selecting a stock to use in all of the different indicator examples was quite a problem. Not that it was difficult to find a good one, most work quite well with the filtering concept. The problem was in maintaining credibility so that you would not think that the universe was combed looking for the perfect example. Therefore, it was decided to use the first stock in both lists of the S&P 100 and the Dow Industrials, Alcoa (AA). Figure 8-5 shows a high-low bar chart of Alcoa along with a histogram of its volume for the period of analysis used in the following examples.

Figure 8-5

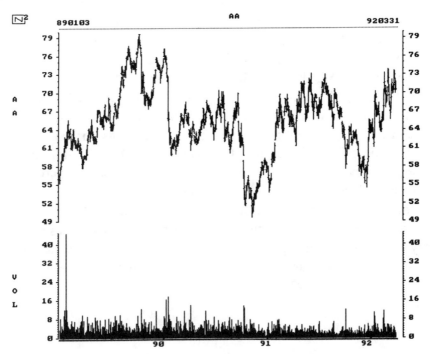

In Figures 8-6 through 8-18, thirteen different indicators are displayed above the candlestick chart of AA. The chart displays only the latest 140 trading days, but the trading analysis still covers the data beginning January 1, 1989, and ending March 31, 1992 (3-1/4 years). The up and down arrows at the top of the chart (above the indicator) show the signals given by the indicator itself. The up and down arrows below the indicator are the automatic candle pattern identification arrows showing each candle pattern and whether it is bullish (up arrow) or bearish (down arrow). If the candle pattern arrow is shown with a double head, it represents a filtered candle pattern. The box in the lower right corner of the chart displays the trading information for the three trading methods. The information in the box shows the effective dates, the total percentage gain or loss, the number of trading signals, and the average percentage gain or loss per trade. You will note that the trading results of the candle patterns by themselves will be the same for all examples. The data did not change, therefore the candle patterns are the same. Only the indicator and, therefore, the filtered candle patterns will change with each example. For all indicator examples, the total gain using candle patterns alone for trading Alcoa (AA) was 45.8% over the period from January 3, 1989, to March 31, 1992. There were 40 trades, which made the average gain per trade equal to 1.14%.

The price of Alcoa on the first day, January 3, 1989, was 55.875 and on the last day, March 31, 1992, was 70.5. So that you will have a basis for judgment, a buy and hold strategy would have yielded slightly more than 26%. Again, neither calculations for commissions nor execution slippage have been figured, nor have the figures been annualized. Because the trading strategy has been kept so simple, one must consider only the relative values when viewing these concepts.

One more thing might not be obvious: all trading is figured up to the value of the closing price on the last day of the data. This does not necessarily mean that a trading signal occurred on that day, only that the percentage gain or loss was calculated as if a valid signal had been given.

Figure 8-6 shows the %D indicator for 14 days, using threshold values of 20 and 80 for the trading signals. The total gain for the filtered candlesticks was not significantly different from that for the indicator alone. However, the number of trades was significantly reduced, bringing the average gain per trade for the filtered candles up to 4.79%, in other words, over 100% better than the indicator.

Chart 8-7 shows the faster %K indicator for 14 days using threshold values of 20 and 80. The difference between %K and %D is only that %D reacts slightly slower than %K. Remember, %D is just a three period moving average of %K. In this example, the filtered candles were over three times better than %K when looking at the average gain per trade.

Figure 8-6

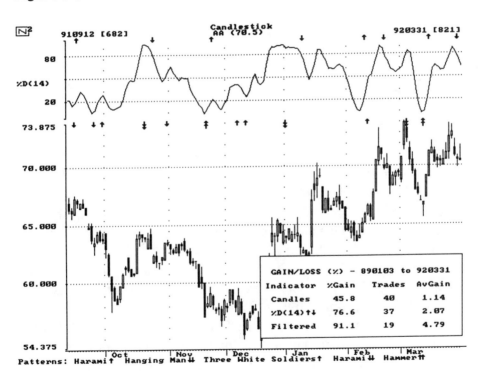

GAIN/LOSS (%) – 890103 to 920331			
Indicator	%Gain	Trades	AvGain
Candles	45.8	40	1.14
%D(14)↑↓	76.6	37	2.07
Filtered	91.1	19	4.79

Patterns: Harami↑ Hanging Man↓↓ Three White Soldiers↑ Harami↓↓ Hammer↑↑

Figure 8-7

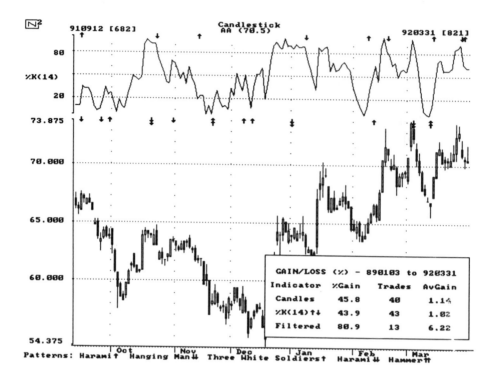

Since %K reacts quicker than %D, one could lower the upper threshold and raise the lower threshold to give a larger filtering area. This would normally generate more trades. For example, by changing the thresholds to 25 and 75, the filtered candles gained 71.6%, with 21 trades for an average gain per trade of 3.41%. Using a larger filtering area was not quite as good as the original example, however, because although it did, in fact, increase the number of trades it did not increase the overall gain. The results of the indicator %K were only slightly improved to 51.9%. Opening up the thresholds to 30 and 70 increased the filtered candle trades to 27 with a gain of only 31.5%. The indicator actually decreased in performance to 45.6%. This shows that the tighter thresholds of 20 and 80 tend to produce

Figure 8-8

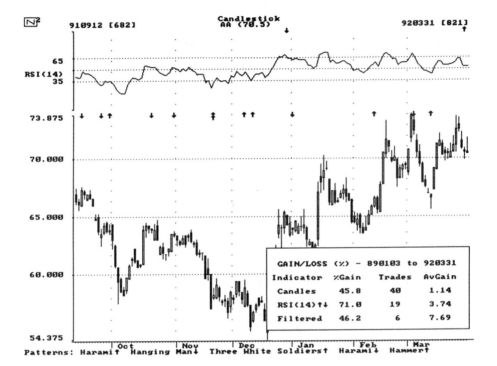

better results for filtering without changing the indicator results appreciably.

Figure 8-8 shows Wilder's RSI for 14 days, with threshold values of 35 and 65. The average gain for the filtered candles was over twice as good as the average gain from RSI. When you consider that there were also fewer trades, the average gain per trade for the filtered candles was exceptionally better than RSI.

Figure 8-9 shows the money flow index. Money flow is calculated similarly to RSI, but the days when the price closes higher are averaged separately from the days when the price closes lower. In this case a period of 21 days was used for the smoothing of both the up closes and the down closes. Prior to smoothing, the change in price each day is multiplied by the volume for that day. This way an up day with large volume would cause a larger move in the indicator than would a similar up day with little volume. Once the two averages are calculated, they are further operated upon to produce an indicator that moves between 0 and 100.

As you can see from the trading box in Figure 8-9, the filtering concept once again performs much better than the indicator itself, even though the indicator did quite well.

Figure 8-9

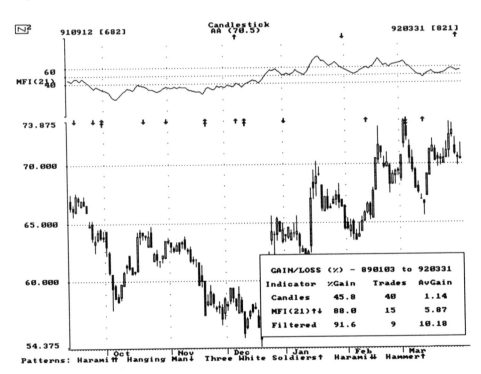

Figure 8-10

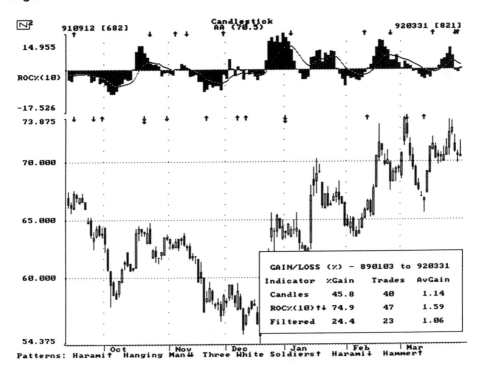

Figure 8-10 shows an indicator knows as the rate of change. Rate of change is a fairly simple concept that is widely used by many analysts. Here a ten-day rate of change is used by taking the percentage difference between the closing price today and the closing price ten days ago. For example, if the value of the rate of change indicator were 7.5, one could deduce that the price on that day was 7.5% greater than the price ten days ago.

The trading signals for this indicator cannot be given by thresholds because the up and down values are theoretically unlimited. Therefore, the trading signals are generated by the crossing of the indicator with its own ten period smoothing. Ten periods for the smoothing value is used for most indicators that work this way. Better values may exist for certain stocks or commodities, but ten seems to be consistently good.

The rate of change indicator did better than the candle patterns and much better than the filtered patterns when looking at total gain. Because the filtered candles almost always result in fewer trades, the average gain was better with the indicator, but not significantly so. The filtering area occurs after the indicator crosses the zero line and before the indicator crosses its own smoothing.

Figure 8-11 shows Arms' Ease of Movement Indicator for 13 periods. The signal is generated when it crosses its own ten period smoothing. Ease of Movement is a numerical method used to quantify the shape of a box used in Equivolume charting. Arms takes a ratio of the box width to the box height, called the box ratio, which is a ratio of the volume to the price range. Heavy volume days with the same price range result in a higher box ratio and, therefore, difficult movement.

Figure 8-11

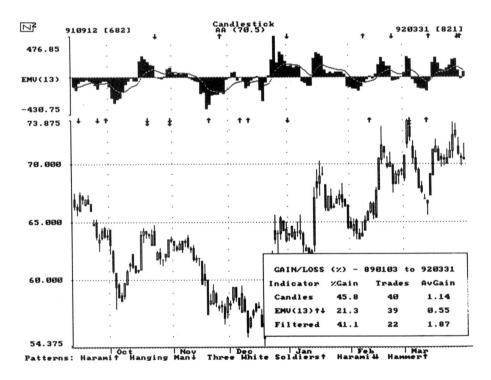

Based upon total gain, this indicator did not do better than candles alone or filtered candles. Likewise, when the number of trades is considered, filtered candles did much better.

Figure 8-12 shows the double momentum oscillator for 18 periods. Like most oscillators, a signal is generated when it crosses its own 10-day smoothing. The double momentum oscillator is a combination of two rate of change calculations which are 20% above and below the value set for the indicator. In this example, the indicator value is set at 18, so the two rate of change calculations are 14 and 22.

In this example, the filtered candles greatly outperformed the indicator.

Figure 8-12

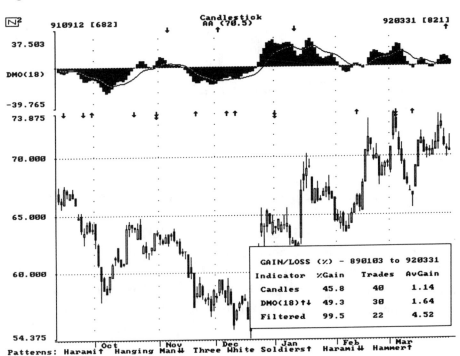

Figure 8-13

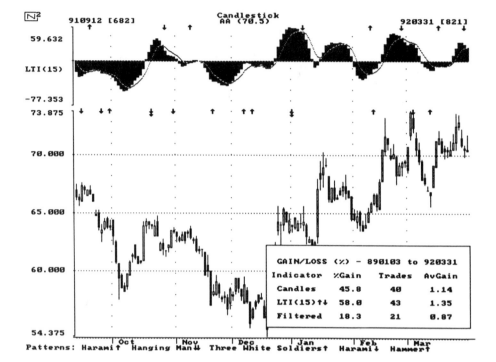

Figure 8-13 shows the linear trend indicator for 15 periods. The linear trend indicator is based upon the slope of a least squares fit over the chosen period, in this case 15 days. Because the LTI is such a smooth line, a shorter 5-day crossover smoothing was used.

From the trading box in Figure 8-13, the indicator generated good results, but the filtering concept failed to do better than the indicator or the candles. Filtered candlesticks obviously does not work every time.

Figure 8-14

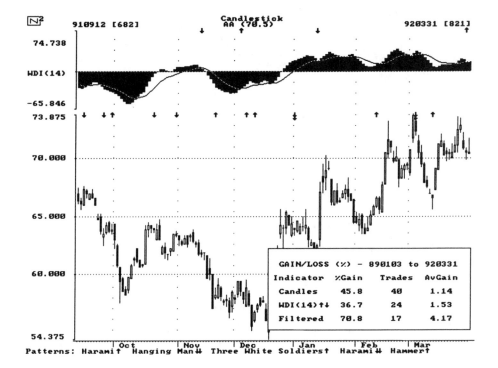

Figure 8-14 shows Wilder's Directional Index for 14 periods. Again, signals are generated when it crosses its own 10-day smoothing. Wilder developed the directional index along with the RSI in 1978 (see bibliography). Using signals from a simple crossover smoothing is not the method Wilder suggested for its use. However, that was the only method that would generate a filtering area.

The filtering concept did quite well here also. Notice that even though the indicator did not do very well, the filtered candles did almost three times better.

Figure 8-15

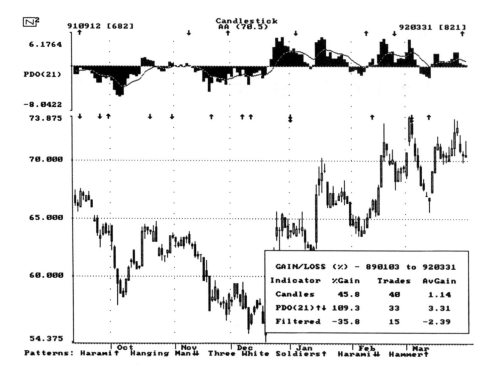

Figure 8-15 shows the price detrend oscillator for 21 periods. This indicator is the difference between the closing price and a smoothing of the closing price, in this case 21 days. Signals are generated when PDO crosses its own 10-period smoothing.

Here is an example where the indicator was exceptional and the filtered candles were a failure. The suspected problem is in defining the filtering area used on the indicator.

Figure 8-16 shows Appel's Moving Average Convergence Divergence Indicator, known as MACD. MACD is an extension of the price detrend

Figure 8-16

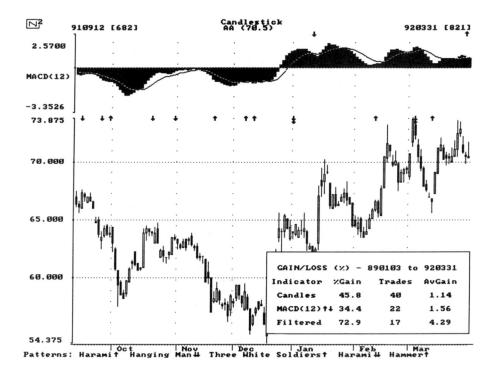

oscillator, in that another smoothed value is used instead of the closing price. MACD uses the difference between a 12-day smoothing and a 25-day smoothing. Signals are generated when this difference crosses its own 9-day smoothing. Nine days were used here because that is the popular setting used by most analysts. Incidentally, in keeping with the previous use of 10 days for the smoothing value, it actually improved the indicator trading results by over 7%.

MACD did not perform well in this example. However, filtered candles yielded an average of 4.29% per trade.

Figure 8-17

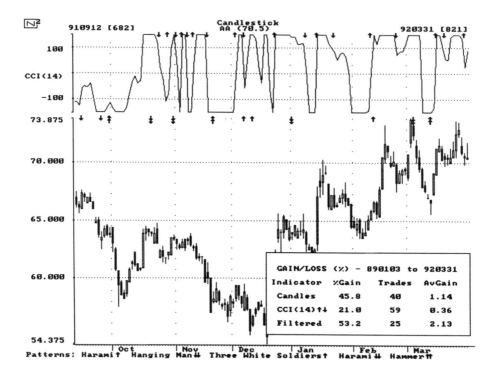

Figure 8-17 shows Lambert's Commodity Channel Index for 14 periods. Signals are given whenever CCI crosses the thresholds of 100 and -100. The Commodity Channel Index was designed for use with commodities that exhibit cyclical and/or seasonal characteristics. It consists of the mean deviation over the number of periods selected, in this case, 14.

Filtered candles, again, did exceptionally well when compared to the indicator or candle patterns.

Figure 8-18

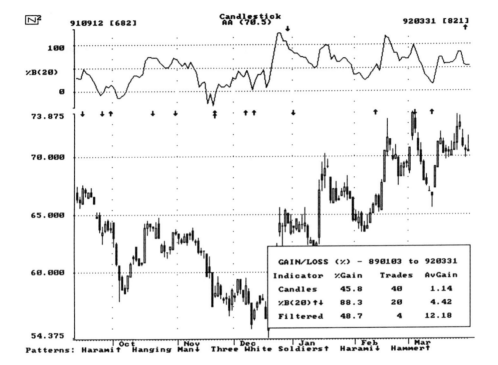

Figure 8-18 shows Bollinger's Oscillator, %B, for 20 periods. %B is another method of displaying the Bollinger Bands developed by John Bollinger. Bollinger Bands used two standard deviations over a period of 20 days to encase about 95% of the price action. It is an excellent way to show the volatility of the market. %B looks merely at the closing price relative to the upper and lower Bollinger Bands, much in the same way as stochastics are calculated. %B is a measure of where the closing price is relative to the Bollinger Bands. Signals are generated whenever %B exceeds 100% and 0%

From the trading box in Figure 8-18, you can see that %B by itself gives excellent trading results, but when used as a filter for candle patterns, the results for average gain are even better.

Chapter 8

Conclusion

It should be obvious that filtering candle patterns with popular indicators is an almost certain method of improving your trading results. Not only does it provide better overall gains from a simple trading system, it will almost always reduce the number of trades. Reducing the amount of trading will also reduce transaction costs and produce a much higher average gain per trade. Filtering works!

9 | Derivative Charting Methods

Candlestick charting has produced a number of derivative charting and analysis methods. The appeal of candlestick charts, as a method of plotting market data, is that they visually help to interpret the market. Your brain can quickly assimilate the information because it is displayed so consistently well. A new charting method, called CandlePower charting, adds a new dimension to candlestick charts: volume. CandlePower is a trademark of N-Squared Computing, the originator of the concept.

CandlePower Charting

CandlePower Charting is another visually appealing charting technique that combines the power of Japanese candlesticks and volume.

Typical charting (whether bar or candlestick) shows the price action on the vertical scale and time on the horizontal scale (see Chapter 1). Volume is usually depicted as a histogram plot under the prices. Two significant pieces of information are generated each time a transaction occurs between a buyer and a seller. One of these, price change, we tend to react to emotionally, and the other, volume, we largely ignore. Volume is certainly a more valuable tool to market analysis than is usually acknowledged. Richard Arms claims that price tells us what is happening and volume tells us how it is happening. Joseph Granville filled an entire career analyzing and writing about volume.

Volume, during most phases of the market, will precede prices. This is a hotly contested remark, but watching both price and volume can only enhance your timing and decision making. Simply said, when price and volume are increasing, it is considered bullish. Likewise, when prices and volume are decreasing, it is considered bearish.

Figure 9-1

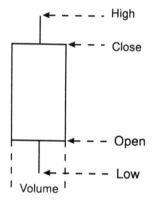

As shown in Figure 9-1, the body of a CandlePower day, just like a candlestick, is made up of the difference between the open and close. The color of the body and the shadows also follow the same conventions used in Japanese candlestick charting. The difference is that the width of the body is a reflection of the volume for that day. A day with large volume will be a wider candlestick body than a day with less volume. On a chart, it is easy to pick out the largest volume day by finding the widest body. Likewise, the day with the smallest volume will be the thinnest body.

Many candle patterns can have added importance when volume is introduced. For instance, a bullish Engulfing Day will be even more bullish if the second day also is accompanied by larger volume. A Morning Star pattern can be judged more successful if there is excessive volume on the last day.

Examples

Figure 9-2

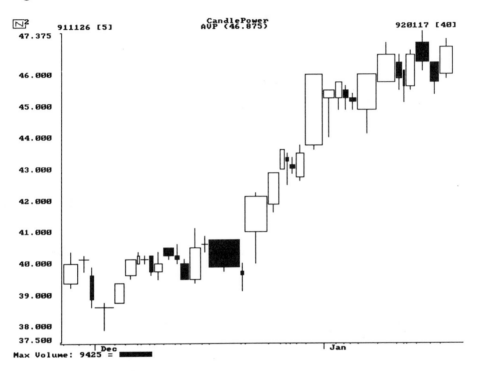

In Figure 9-2, the CandlePower chart of Avon Products (AVP), notice how the upmove contains large white candle lines. These wide lines show that the upmove is fully supported by volume. Once the large white days dry up, the move has probably run its course.

The large black day in the chart of Bell South (BEL) shows a classic volume blow-off day (Figure 9-3). After a good upmove, the volume starts to dry up. Then, in one day, prices explode to the upside, but close near their lows on very large volume. A few days into the decline, a three-day rally is terminated with a gap down. Then the decline continues.

Figure 9-3

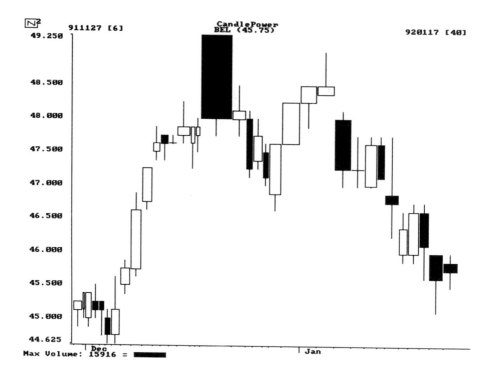

In Figure 9-4, the chart of Citicorp (CCI), notice how each turning point in the market is accompanied by large volume. The market bottomed with a large black day, then rallied. The rally stopped with a large white day, then went sideways until the next large white day. From there it gapped up twice, followed by two days of indecision (Spinning Tops), each with large volume. Here again, Spinning Tops with large volume support the indecision of the marketplace. Large amounts of stock changed hands, but no side took the leadership.

Figure 9-4

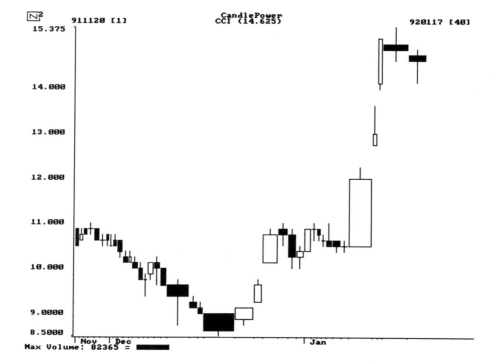

The bottom reversal toward the end of December on the chart of Litton (LIT) shows continually larger-volume days (Figure 9-5). In fact, if it were not for the small white Spinning Top day, a Morning Star bullish reversal pattern would have represented the bottom. Here is another example where volume increasing throughout a pattern will add to its significance.

Figure 9-6, the last example of CandlePower charting, shows more data (volume maximum has been reduced), so the richness of the charting method can be fully appreciated.

Figure 9-5

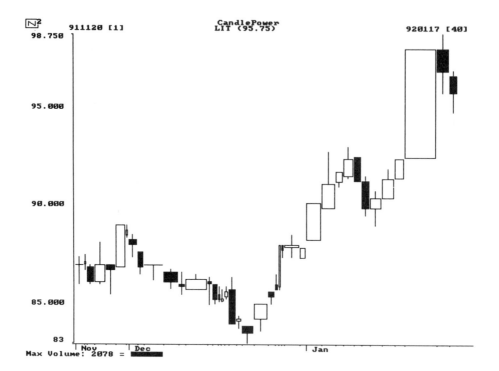

Figure 9-6

Condensed CandlePower Charting

Another twist is added to CandlePower charting with Condensed CandlePower charting. In this approach, the time element is returned to the horizontal axis. The variable-width candlestick bodies are still displayed accurately, but they overlap. Each new day starts at a uniform distance (time) interval. This method of charting displays more data at once, while still giving the large-volume days visibility. Individual candle patterns are more difficult to see, though.

Areas of volume congestion can be easily spotted using condensed CandlePower Charting. Trendlines used on this type of chart would also reflect the volume component.

Example

Figure 9-7

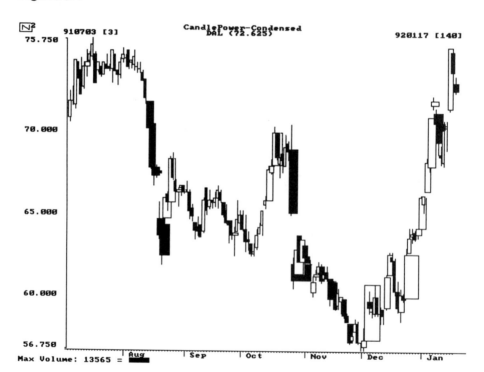

The data used for the Condensed CandlePower chart in Figure 9-7 is the same as in the last example of CandlePower Charting. This was done intentionally, so you could easily see the difference in charting methods.

10 | Conclusion

Successful analysis of the stock and futures markets is not an easy task. Most participants prepare themselves no better than they would for a game of cards. One must first learn how these markets work, then learn about the many different kinds of analysis that are available, such as, fundamental and technical analysis. On a smaller scale, the field of technical analysis offers a host of varying techniques; Japanese candlestick analysis is one of these.

Throughout this book, it was emphasized that candlestick analysis should be used with other analysis methods. At the risk of sounding contradictory, I would like to warn that too many methods can only confuse and hinder. It reminds me of the saying that the person with a watch always knows what time it is, but the person with two watches is never sure.

It has been shown that candle pattern analysis can enhance the use and timing of popular technical indicators. Filtered candlesticks consistently outperform a host of technical indicators and usually candle patterns by themselves. The combination of technical indicators and techniques is not new; in fact, it is the method of analysis most successful traders use. Adding candle patterns to that arsenal will surely further improve trading results.

I'm sure that with the passing of time, new and different analysis techniques will surface. Some will gain in popularity, some will go by the wayside. Any analysis technique that has a substantial basis for its method will usually survive. I am convinced that candlestick charting and candle pattern analysis will be a survivor.

CandlePower Software

All of the charts, the candle pattern ranking, and filter testing was accomplished with a software program called CandlePower by N-Squared Systems. CandlePower software will *automatically* identify all 62 of the patterns mentioned in this book. Complete filtering capability on the following listed indicators is quickly and easily accomplished:

- **Arms' Ease of Movement**

- **Price Detrend Oscillator**

- **Wilder's RSI**

- **Lambert's Commodity Channel Index**

- **Bollinger's Oscillator**

- **Wilder's Directional Indicator**

- **Lane's Stochastics**

- **Double Momentum Oscillator**

- **Price Rate of Change**

- **Appel's MACD**

- **Linear Trend Indicator**

- **Money Flow Index**

- **Plus, Expert Signal Predictor**

Expert Signal Predictor will combine the power of any or all of the trading indicators to provide accurate and timely trading signals. Expert Signal Predictor comes set with extensively tested and proven parameters so that you need only turn on your computer to begin using its expert predictions. Or, if you like to experiment with ideas and parameters of your own, or don't like a particular indicator, drop it, change it, control its weighting, or test it. Reset it anytime you like. You can see Expert Signal Predictor change with each adjustment you make. Despite its ease of use, Expert Signal Predictor is not a black box, it is explained in detail in the documentation that accompanies the software.

If you would like a software package that does all of the analysis discussed in this book, N-Squared Systems will extend a special offer to you. Upon proof of purchase of this book, you will get a $50 discount on the CandlePower software from N-Squared Systems. If you would like a fully functional demo program, N-Squared Systems will send it to you, upon request, at no charge.

N-Squared Systems
6821 Lemongrass Loop SE
Salem, OR 97306

Appendix

An interview with Japanese trader, Mr. Takehiro Hikita

Mr. Takehiro Hikita has graciously provided me with a large amount of insight into the candle pattern philosophy. I have never met anyone so devoted to the detailed study of a concept as he. He started using candlestick analysis many years ago, in fact, all of his charting was done by hand until personal computers became available.

During a trip to Japan in January, 1992, I studied the candle philosophy and interpretation with Mr. Hikita. I also maintained a log of our conversations, from which I have selected appropriate questions for this interview.

Occasional editing was done to assist in clarifying his answers, definitely not to change the meaning. It became quite obvious to me, that using English as a second language resulted in a completely honest and direct response; with no effort to be clever or entertaining. I found this to be quite refreshing and decided that you might also.

1. **How and when did you first become interested in investing and trading?**

   I believe it was when I was around 31 years of age, that is over 25 years ago. It was, however, once terminated and I stayed out of the market for about 2 years after losing money, more than enough at that time.

2. **When did you realize that a form of technical analysis was better than fundamental analysis?**

It was when I started trading again and I was around 41 years of age, after leaving the company for some reason. Beginning with the candlestick pattern analysis, I studied and researched all different kinds of Japanese analysis techniques with real trading, and was extended later on to the method available in the States. My starting to trade again was with the policy to do so based on the technical analysis and no more guesses and fundamental analysis to make a living. I am fortunately still in the business of trading.

Speaking of this story a little further I started subscribing Commodities (now called Futures) and purchased many publications such as Commodity Trading Systems and Methods written by Kaufman and Wilder's publications. My first use of a calculator was the programmable Texas Instruments product on Wilder's method. Then the Casio's programmable calculator for me to build in my own method, as I became serious. Then to make the daily analysis much easier, I purchased the IBM-5100 with 32K memory; it was in 1977.

In 1979, I learned the Apple II came out on the market which has a graphic capability. I then immediately purchased it by importing direct from the States. In 1980, I joined CompuTrac and attended their first TAG Conference in New Orleans. My Stock & Commodities magazine subscription started since then.

3. **Did you always use candle charting for your analysis? If not, when did you start using candle charts?**

It was from the very beginning, as far as taking a look at the market in general, to know how the market is acting. Since the candlestick charting method is the only one available in Japan to record the history of the price activity in graphic form. It is just like the bar chart in the States. Regardless whether I liked it or not, it was what was used then.

But, the candlestick pattern analysis is another subject, rather than the charting itself. My interest on how to read the pattern better was probably few years later. I first started trading after reading the first issue of Shimuzu's book in 1965, the original of The Japanese Chart of Charts translated by Nicholson.

4. Are candles used in Japan today as widely as bar charts are used in the USA?

As already mentioned in the above, there is no other method than candlestick charting to show a market record and activity in Japan. Yes, it is being used just like the bar chart in the States. The pattern recognition is another subject within the chart analysis.

5. Is the word candlestick a Western term? If so, what is candle charting and analysis called in Japan?

There is generally nothing but the candlestick charting to show the trend and market activity, and any others are classified as the analysis since they are rather clear to know the pinpoint to take an action, like the Point & Figure chart. Speaking of the chart, we generally call it Hi Ashi / Daily Chart, Shu Ashi / Weekly Chart, and Tsuki Ashi / Monthly Chart. The Japanese word for candle is roshoku.

For your information, Ashi means Leg or better say Foot, and the foot has an inside meaning of the past record, that is probably from the foot stamp that shows the past movement and activities, not only as a market term but in general. I then feel the Candlefoots is better to be called in English. It is, however, alright as long as understandable and sounds smooth to you people's ears.

6. Do you trade stocks, futures, or both?

Yes, I trade both. I trade actively the futures but not the stocks. My trading stock is a long term basis, never sale, that is in order to hedge from inflation, while trading the future is to make money in the short term.

There is other reason, it is easier to find a pivot in the futures, especially to find out a pinpoint to short and I like to sell, rather than long, which has a false start often, compared to going short. Not only that, it will be only one third of time needed for movement to gain the same price difference in case of short, against in case of long.

7. **Have you found that candles work better with stocks, futures, or does it matter?**

Again, the candles chart and candles pattern analysis should be separated. The candlestick is only the chart itself, but the candlestick patterns are the analysis based generally on the Sakata's Five Law, or somehow originating from it. There are two applications in the law, one for daily and the other is for weekly chart which has a different definition. The daily candlesticks pattern works better on the futures. It is again because of speed, the futures has a short trend cycle while the stocks is longer.

8. **Which candle patterns seem to work best for you? Can you list your ten favorite patterns?**

Your question is too straightforward even though it might be scientific approach to research, so it is awfully difficult to answer it. You have to understand that the candle patterns analysis is originating from man's experience in trading, and that is a mix of market tendency with the human psychology expressed in the pattern. There is no scientific logic at all.

Approaching from a statistic viewpoint and supposing there were 100% perfect patterns, if it comes once a year, or about one every three years, nobody can keep watching to see it and catch it. It must be based on such a daily analysis, repeating tedious business. There is, also, no guarantee that a pattern showed 100% successful in the past, will work well repeatedly in future. In statistical speaking, the number of the sample is the important factor and so it can not be compared with other in a different number of sampling.

I would like to see a research report that will be able to do by your software, or will be done by somebody else. Again, it will be all differ-

ent results by each software even though using exactly the same data because of the definition used by every software program. They will each be a little bit different in defining the patterns, along with definition of filtering to define it. So any such research report should be with a note within this program and within that program, not as a candle pattern itself. It is the matter of the pattern quality inside software other than the system quality.

In conclusion, I should say it always depends on how used, in conjunction with others and market condition such as how many counts in new high or new low included, but not by candlestick pattern itself. Again, the candle pattern is one of the analysis tools.

9. **Which candle patterns do you think are not very good? How about a list?**

Again, my answer will be the same as the above explained. It depends upon the market condition and the price level and so on.

10. **Do you trade or make timing decisions based solely on candle patterns or do you use them in conjunction with other technical indicators?**

Of course I use the candles pattern in conjunction with other technical indicators. As you know there is no perfect technical analysis method by itself, and again the candlestick pattern is also one of them covering some part of the 360 degrees that must be defended. The daily candlestick pattern analysis is, however, good with futures as one of the timing tools. Again, there is nothing that covers all the degrees needed for technical analysis.

It is my intention to make an accent in trading by number of contracts in opening a position, depending upon the market condition, that requires the guts, too, which is another of the factors required. One contract each time without the accent will never let you make money. This is one reason why I am not interested in any of the valuable factors of optimized automated trading systems. They seem to be only playing the game for fun, so I don't like it. Everybody who wants to make money should be aware of no easy money anywhere in the world, unless you are lucky or originated from a son of a king.

Author's Note: Mr. Hikita is referring to trading multiple contracts when the candle signals are supported. Also, he stressed the importance of using the candle pattern signals to assist in opening and closing of positions, not necessarily for reversing positions only.

11. Which indicators have you found that work well with candle patterns?

I have to emphasize, this time, that it depends upon the market condition and the price level which indicator is good to use with the candle patterns. I feel, however, that stochastic %D works fairly good in general, if you can correctly count the cycles and confluence/convergence on different cycle generated by %D. And, pinpointing tops and bottoms using a combination of the stochastic oscillator seems good.

12. Candlestick analysis is growing rapidly in the United States. Do you think that it is just a fad or do you think candle analysis is here to stay?

I suppose it is a not fad and will stay long in the States. Because this way of expression of the market has much advantage in comparing it to the bar chart, so that it is easier to understand the daily price change. There is also another good point, for instance it has a open price mark, that we understand important factor to read the market. Also, it is easy to know by one quick look at candle which way the market moved during the day. Since each pattern has a deep meaning similar to Gann analysis, it will last a long time within traders who are interested in the philosophy behind the patterns.

13. What advice would you offer to Western traders about candlestick analysis?

To understand the candle patterns you should understand the philosophy inside and behind each pattern. Since it is not a perfect technique, as is the same case with others, it is also important not to depend solely on the patterns itself, but use it in conjunction with others based on a logically established method. The candle pattern analysis is one of the analysis methods that was built up by human impression and expressed by image from the combination of the pattern based on history. Beyond a maximum possible technical analysis there is another world of discipline of the mental power, that is to establish your philosophy.

The candle patterns must be believed in if you get signal, you must execute or follow the market very closely. Stay in touch with each candle signal. If you become disconnected, the psychology behind the candle pattern will not work well.

Once you establish your trading policy, whatever you can believe based on the above explanations, you will not make a big mistake. You will be aware of mistakes in advance within an acceptable level of damage, as long as employing a proper trend analysis. If you had this policy you will be then not disappointed by any accident, and will be able to understand this way the market is wrong, instead of you and your policy, in the case of the market being against you.

Final Note

As you can see from this interview, Mr. Hikita thinks that the separation of candlestick charting and candle pattern analysis is important. Also, one cannot forget the underlying psychology behind each candle pattern. These are insights into the minds of the traders and speculators that move the market every day.

Mr. Hikita always referenced his trading analysis to dancing with the trend. This concept is not new to technical analysts, however, many traders must graduate from the school of bitter experience before they realize its importance.

Bibliography

Analysis of Stock Price in Japan. Tokyo: Nippon Technical Analysts Association, 1988.

Hikita, Takehiro. *Shin Shuu-Ashi Tohshi Hoh — Tohkei to Kakuritsu de Toraeru* (New weekly chart method — based on statistics and probability). IOM Research Publications, 1977.

Hikita, Takehiro. *Daizu no Sekai — Yunyu Daizu no Semekata Mohhekata* (The world of Soybeans — attacking methods on imported soybeans and how to profit from it). IOM Research Publications, 1978.

Kaburagi, Shigeru. *Sakimono Keisen — Sohba Okuno Hosomichi* (Futures charts — explained in a detailed way to be an expert in trading). Tohshi Nipoh Sha, 1991.

Kisamori, Kichitaro. *Kabushiki Keisen no Mikata Tsukaikata — Tohshika no Tameno Senryakuzu* (How to read and apply charts on stocks — Strategies for the investor). Toyo Keizai Shinpoh Sha, 1978.

Lane, George C. *Using Stochastics, Cycles, and RSI.* Des Plaines, IL, 1986.

Bibliography

Murphy, John J. *Technical Analysis of the Futures Markets.* New York: New York Institute of Finance, 1986.

N-Squared Computing. *CandlePower 3 Software Manual.* Silverton, OR, 1992.

Nison, Steve. *Japanese Candlestick Charting Techniques.* New York: New York Institute of Finance, 1991.

Obunsha's Essential Japanese-English Dictionary. Japan, 1990.

Ohyama, Kenji. *Inn-Yoh Rohsoku-Ashi no Mikata—Jissenfu ni Yoru* (How to read a black and white / negative and positive candlefoot—In view of the actual record). Japan Chart Co., Ltd., 1986.

Sakata Goho wa Fuurin Kazan—Sohba Keisen no Gokui (The Sakata Rules are wind, forest, fire, and mountain): 2nd updated 3rd ed. Nihon Shohken Shimbun Sha, 1991.

> Author's note: The above reference was an excellent source for many of the candle patterns. The name Fuurin Kazan may be translated as *Fu*—the speed like wind, *Rin*—that quietness like forest, *Ka*—that battle like fire, and *Zan*—that immobile position like mountain. This idiom originated from the Chinese battle strategy that Honma was said to have read.

Shimizu, Seiki. *The Japanese Chart of Charts.* Tokyo: Toyko Futures Trading Publishing Co., 1986.

Wilder, J. Welles, Jr. *New Concepts in Technical Trading Systems.* Greensboro, NC: Trend Research, 1978.

Yasui, Taichi. *Kabushiki Keisen no Shinzui—Nichi Bei Keisen Bunseki no Subete* (A picture of the stock chart). Tokyo: Toyo Keizai Shinpoh Sha, 1981.

Yatsu, Toshikazu. *Tensai Shohbashi "Honma Shohkyu Hiden" —Kabu Hisshoh Jyutsu* (A genius trader Sohkyu Honma into his secret — To be confident of victory on stock investments). Diamond Sha, 1990.

Yoshimi, Toshihihko. *Toshihiko Yoshimi no Chato Kyoshitsu* (A classroom on charting). Japan Chart Co., Ltd., 1991.

Index

Index

Index

Index

ABOUT THE AUTHOR

Gregory L. Morris is President of G. Morris Corporation, an investment/software consulting firm headquartered in Dallas, Texas. He provides technical consultation in the area of investment analysis, technical analysis and software development. Mr. Morris received his B.S. in Aerospace Engineering from the University of Texas in Austin. Upon graduating, he attended Officer Candidate School, Jet Pilot Training and Navy Fighter Weapons School (Top Gun), and also flew F4 Phantom jets aboard the aircraft carrier U.S.S. Independence. Mr. Morris is the author of several articles for *Technical Analysis of Stocks and Commodities* magazine and has appeared many times as guest speaker on Financial News Network.